The Tyrin Chronicles

The Tyrin Chronicles

...THEY ARE COMING

A Novel By

NICOLE NiBLACK MONTOYA

MILL CITY PRESS

Xulon Press
2301 Lucien Way #415
Maitland, FL 32751
407.339.4217
www.xulonpress.com

Cover Photograph & Design: Aldred W. Montoya
Editor: Jessica Bryan, www.oregoneditor.com

THE IYRIN CHRONICLES

Paperback ISBN-13: 978-1-6628-1555-3
Ebook ISBN-13: 978-1-6628-155-60

This Book Is Dedicated To

Almighty God

My Beloved Husband Aldred Wesley Montoya

My parents B. Jean & John Louis Niblack

My siblings Jonathan Niblack & Sydney Cowie

and my precious ElfnTru

To my dearest friends
Kara Nakfoor / Psychic Reader and Healer

Ramie Reed and my editor Jessica Bryan, without whose
combined intuitive insights, encouragement and professional
guidance the task could not have been completed.

- NNM

The Iyrin Speak

"We, the Iyrin are creations of Our Father, and we
are more in number than Man's mind can imagine.
Yes, there were those, more than two hundred by your count,
who followed the first who fell from Grace.
There were those who were disobedient to My Father's will
to preserve the Earth for the flowering of Man.
And those who would taint Mankind with their seed
and with wisdoms that Man was not yet meant to have.
For you were My Father's children. Not ours.
Yes – some did fall – but not all. Not most.
Not enough to be but less than a speck in My Father's eye.
And now their essence returns
unto the Earth to take vengeance through Man.
This is why we have been sent to observe, to lament for Man
will decide his own fate. We are but Watchers."

– The Arch Amun

Introduction

The *Iyrin Chronicles* is a mystical work, a book of prophecy that speaks to the human heart in response to the troubles of humanity and the transition we are facing.

So ... who, or what, are The Iyrin of which this book speaks? Men have called them "angels," the ones who returned to Earth from heaven, sent by The Creator to provide guidance and comfort to mankind, as we suffer through the present and coming changes caused by loss, illness, the corruption of the Earth, and other planetary shifts that are to come. Their purpose is to ensure humankind does not sink into utter madness and despair during these unprecedented times, and eradicate themselves completely from the sight of God.

A new form of man is soon to be born upon the Earth – a "just" species – children of The Father, whom The Iyrin will serve to protect from those among men who would see them destroyed.

1

In the Beginning There Was ... the End

Matthew hated God. He hated God and he didn't give a damn who knew it. After the catastrophe that happened to him and the rest of the world three years before, an event most could only bring themselves to call "The Incident," or "*that* day". Questioning the existence of God was considered some extremely dodgy, if not potentially life-altering business. This was because there was no longer a question as to whether or not God existed.

Three years ago, the existence of the living God had become an irrefutable fact to every man, woman and child upon the Earth. Every sentient being upon the planet came to know simultaneously, without a shadow of a doubt, that God was most assuredly a very real factor in their lives. Mankind had also been granted the privilege of learning not only was God a force to be reckoned with – albeit cautiously – but there was also no longer any hesitation on the part of the said Divinity to mete out swift reprisals upon those who dared commit an affront to His existence. This was the God made manifest in the minds of men, women, and children around the globe, in place of the omnipotent and benevolent, well-aged, grey-bearded figure of olde that Humankind had held in their collective hearts and minds for millennia.

And it had been this God who wiped Matthew Knightly's single passion for living out of existence as simply and swiftly as any schoolteacher erases the chalky remnants from a blackboard at the end of a day's lesson.

In short, the God Matthew was raised from childhood to know had turned out to be, by all accounts, an intangible bully who was not above or beyond perpetuating the sorrows and mostly self-imposed miseries of Humankind for His own closely kept, and as of yet, unrevealed purpose. That much, at least, humanity had become used to living with long before the day of The Great Reveal ... The Earth Event ... or whatever else one chose to call it to make it easier for them to sleep at night.

Whenever Matthew closed his eyes, which wasn't often these days, he could clearly see the smiling face of his five-year-old daughter, Maia Joy, whom he affectionately called "My Joy," for that is what she was to him. Her tiny perfectly square teeth, flashed like pieces of impossibly white, miniature Chiclets gum in the bright sunlight of his memory. Her full, smooth lips were blood flushed and velvety soft like a ripened peach. He would often recall the day when she was born and the moment he saw her flawlessly formed lips for the first time. For they had been nothing less than two tiny red ochre-colored flower petals, idyllically folded like an unopened orchid bloom.

He had briefly toyed with the idea of naming his only child "Orchid," after the exotic plant, but her mother squashed the idea in a rather short and firm order. And now (or should it be it then?) ...he was becoming more and more confused as to how to measure time.

He was even less certain as to when he was awake and lucid, or whether he had once again been trapped in the moment of horror that lay in constant wait for him behind his eyelids...a horror which had taken place three years and fourteen days before and would be forever etched in his mind. Yes...he was sure this was how he should remember it, in days. But in truth, he did not want to remember it, at all. No. Not. At. All.

Three years and two weeks ago, he had brought his precious Maia to the place where he now stood, a park locally known as "The Point," a roughly twelve-acre, man-made grassy peninsula on the South Side of Chicago that jutted out about a tenth of a mile over Lake Michigan. The park offered one of the few unobstructed and stunning northerly views of the city's famous skyline. It had been an exceptionally sunny day on that Saturday afternoon in late August. The weather had not been exactly warm; after all, it was Chicago, a place where nearly every day of the year carried a cool breeze. But nevertheless, the sun seemed determined to have her way in the sky. And what little warmth she was able to muster served to blast away any clouds that dared to challenge her.

The sky had been so still and blue, and Matthew remembered thinking it looked as surreal as any David Hockney painting he had ever seen.

In his mind's eye, he remembered standing near the center of the park, surrounded by a lush carpet of freshly cut grass, still shockingly green so late in the year. The pseudo meadow hosted a generous spattering of individuals and diversified family units of varying ages, who had also brought their children to enjoy the day. Some of the adults tossed soft rubber balls back and forth to their children, while others gleefully chased what were presumably, smaller generations of themselves as they giggled and ran here and there for the simple joy of racing the wind.

A young Chinese woman was repeatedly folding her arms around her toddler son and rolling in the grass as happily as a couple of frolicking horses cooling themselves off in the dust of a hot afternoon. The little boy squealed with high-pitched delight whenever his mother released him briefly, before scooping him up again to repeat the game.

Matthew remembered how it felt to embrace an armful of giggles, and a memory abruptly brought his inner eye back to the visage of himself standing in the middle of the park with Maia held up high in his outstretched hands. He was holding her firmly, securely, under her narrow armpits, as he suspended her in midair above his head.

The memory of what followed assaulted his mind and he shuddered. In less than a millisecond, his baby girl's chest would put forth a barrage of giggles and his heart would nearly burst with sorrow. But it was not real, not anymore. It had been real though ... once ... but only once.

His mind abruptly shifted forward in time to three years and two weeks from that day, into the present, and he wondered if he was having what people used to call an "out-of-body" experience. But then, just as suddenly, he was thrust back in time again and into the memory of that horrible day. It did not matter that he was unable to put a name to what was happening to him because now Maia was with him. The crisp, fresh air coming off the lake filled his nostrils and lungs, and he could clearly see his five-year-old daughter dressed in her favorite purple jumper, which had large, audacious white flowers screen-printed all over it. She had insisted upon wearing it, despite it being far too late in the year to do so without a set of thermal underwear underneath.

Matthew saw himself holding her high in the air as they played her favorite "Daddy's Game." This is what she had called any silly activity he devised to amuse her. This game usually involved him hoisting her off the ground in some fashion or other, and it was almost certain to cause her to squeal in youthful delight. And on this day – that day – the last day – the only day that mattered – the game had been "helicopter."

The sun was so bright as he twirled his baby girl around and around, all the while looking up into her face and drowning in her. In or out of his body, in the past or the present, wherever he was, the vision was tangible enough to make his eyes water from the stark memory of the sunlight that remained a constant in his mind's eye. This part at least was real, wasn't it? He didn't have to touch the face of his future self to know it was wet with tears.

He scrutinized the memory of himself, thinking about how skinny he looked in the pair of "yeah, I might have been in the Marines once" camouflaged pants that hung loosely from his narrow waist. These well-worn pants that once belonged to his father were just about all that remained of the man who had left his wife and eight-year-old son to fight and die for his country somewhere in a desert in the Middle East.

Matthew knew he would never be able to fit into his father's pants properly, either mentally or physically. Still…they had belonged to his father, and on some days this fact alone was enough to comfort him.

It was somewhat disturbing that he could never readily recall a specific memory of being with his father. Whenever he tried, the only visual that surfaced was that of a nondescript, medium-sized cardboard box. The United States military had shipped this particular box containing his father's personal belongings to Matthew's mother. He and his mother were not home when the box arrived, so the mailman left it sitting in a corner on the porch. It rained heavily in the afternoon and the porch awning was in need of repair. His father had habitually promised to take care of it when he came home.

Of course, the mailman didn't know about the leaky awning, and all that remained of the personal effects of his fallen father were taken into the house in a soggy box smelling of the man Matthew had known, intermingled with wet cardboard and gutter water. He remembered thinking a boy shouldn't have to decipher the kind of man his father had been solely by the wet contents of a medium-sized cardboard box. A man had given his life, a woman her husband and a boy his only father, but the government didn't think any of it was worth the cost of having his dad's things wrapped and delivered properly. In the end, the most vivid memory Matthew had of his father was an aging photo patiently peeled out of that soggy box by his mother.

It was still firmly secured behind the glass of the wooden, five-by-seven picture frame his father had put it in before he took it off to battle with him. The photograph showed the three of them laughing and smiling together the day before his father left to go overseas – for what would be the last time.

Matthew had been a scrawny, six-year-old, gleefully perched atop his father's broad shoulders. He was grinning madly, even though his two front baby teeth were missing. The picture, along with his father's standard issue military portrait, remained firmly rooted on the fireplace mantle in their living room until the day his mother died.

As the years passed, Matthew eventually found solace under the unwavering gaze of the proud, handsome man dressed in his Marine Blues, a man who bore a striking resemblance to the face Matthew was starting to see whenever he looked in a mirror. But it wouldn't be until after the birth of his own child that he would come to understand the many reasons his mother flipped out whenever he whimsically voiced a desire to follow in his father's footsteps and join the Corps.

Yes, now he understood. He had come to understand so much more than was fair for a man of twenty-nine. When his mother died soon after Maia's fourth birthday, Matthew was nearly physically incapacitated with grief. He hadn't realized the depths of his emotional attachment to his mother until she was actually gone. The intensity of his grief caught him off-guard, and only his love for Maia kept him from crawling inside his mother's casket and dying right alongside her.

The feel of his daughter's tiny arms wrapped around his neck as she hugged him also made him rethink a secondary dark notion. That of signing up for an overseas tour of duty or two, with the sole intention of getting himself killed, courtesy of the good ol' U.S. of A. It frightened him to think about the things unfathomable depths of grief can drive a person to contemplate. All in the name of making that terrible, evil, gut- wrenching pain of death and loss subside. But he was far beyond the pain of death now. Three years and two weeks later. Now, he was simply…numb.

He hadn't known at the time of his mother's passing there was something else far worse than the pain caused by the death of someone you loved. It was worse because this "something" was incomplete and without closure. It was the "something" that ate away at your soul each day while slowly consuming whatever remained of your sanity. The descent into that special brand of madness, the kind that lives on the soft underbelly of grief, was not to be rushed.

Your sanity would be drawn from you like a fine rare wine, one small sip at a time, until you ended up either bat-shit-crazy or worse, facilitating or orchestrating your own death, without ever finding an answer as to why the things that happened to you in your miserable life had happened, at all. Maybe the better question was, "Exactly what the fuck happened, anyway?"

Matthew still didn't know the answer to that one, and neither did any of the supposedly top leading scientists in the world. All anyone knew for certain was that "something" had indeed happened. And it happened in every corner of the Earth. The only thing Matthew knew or cared about was that when whatever happened did happen, it happened to Maia.

He suddenly found himself mentally standing once again in the middle of the park. He was back at The Point on that sunny day, holding Maia in his outstretched arms. He could feel her slender frame within the cusp of his hands and the heat underneath her armpits warming the tops of his hands. He swept her up, off her feet, swinging her as high into the air as his strength would allow. He ruminated on the tiny drops of spittle that flew from her mouth and landed on the bridge of his nose as she squealed in childish delight. She tried to catch her breath, but her giggles demanded release.

Matthew felt the warm burst of her sugary breath as it exploded from her narrow torso. Those giggles sounded to him every bit as bubbly as a can of soda pop that has been shaken before being opened to expel the agitated sweetness gurgling within. He could hear the sound of his own laughter mingling with the chime-like laughter of his only child. She was the only tangible thing on this earth that allowed him to see what little good he might have done. This slip of a girl, with her curly brown hair and soft tawny eyes, defined him. She was his anchor, his hope, and his heart. And the tyrant God knew it.

Matthew's memory of the moment his daughter ceased to exist was as clear as any bright and cloudless sky. As clear and bright as the Thursday afternoon when Maia was a living, breathing extension of his outstretched arms. He held her high and turned her around and around, fast enough to set her thick curly hair aflutter in the breeze. Her eyes were wide with excitement and childhood joy. She wasn't afraid; she knew her Daddy would never let her fall. She knew no matter how high or how fast they twirled, her Daddy had her and he would never let her go. He had her. And he did! He did have her!

And then, she...was...gone.

As father and child made one last turn into the crisp wind blowing off the lake, Maia simply ceased to be. Matthew was looking into her sweet face, and then ... he wasn't.

All that was before him now were his own outstretched arms with nothing but an expanse of cloudless blue sky between them – an empty blue sky in the space where a beautiful, five-year-old girl had been only a few seconds earlier. He thought he felt the air around his daughter being sucked away from him.

It was as though she had been harshly snatched sideways into some invisible pocket of air. In that moment, that last horrible, terrifying moment, he could smell the faintest scent of her lingering in the air before it was carried away on a breeze. Matthew felt as if time had stopped. It had actually. For him, anyway.

Perhaps it was because his brain had most certainly been forced to stop as it made a feeble attempt to process what had just happened.

He was keenly aware of feeling his heart pounding madly in his chest – a heart that pounded and thrashed against the walls of his ribcage in an all-out effort to burst free from its fleshy mooring to follow wherever his baby had gone. How did he look, standing in the middle of a patch of grass with both arms outstretched toward the expanse of a cloudless blue sky? His hands spread wide with fingers claw-like and clutching at the memory of the form of a child that was no longer there? He clutched at nothing, his mouth agape and his facial muscles caught between a broad smile and a gut-wrenching grimace that fully illustrated his sudden pain and utter confusion. His child, his Maia, had simply vanished.

It happened so fast that a visual outline of her remained on his retinas. But the illusion was gone with the next proverbial "blinking of the eye."

And no matter how often, or how hard, or how long Matthew frantically blinked in the moments that followed, his Maia never came back. The sudden absence of his daughter brought forth an unbearable sound from his chest.

It wasn't a scream or a wail, but a noise that formed deep within his gut only to burst forth as "Gackt!" And then he screamed. He screamed for her. He screamed at her. He spun around and around in this, his moment of madness, seeking the precious thing he had surely somehow flung across the park! But the park was as wide open an expanse as the sky, a place built for the young to run uninhibited, all while affording their watchful parents the ability to see far and wide.

There literally was no place in the park for a child not to be seen. Matthew's breath hitched in his throat as his brain feverishly tried to make sense out of what had just happened.

He screamed Maia's name and spun around in circles looking for a direction in which to run and search for her. To rescue her if need be. But he could clearly see across the entire park. There were no obstructions, not even a garbage can, only an endless splendor of grass.

Maia wasn't there, and Matthew soon realized there were no longer any children in the park, at all. Out of the forty or so adults remaining in the park, a few were frantically screaming the names of their children while others stood dumbfounded, turning in slow circles and in some cases, looking down at their empty hands in shocked bewilderment.

An elderly woman fainted and lay prostrate on the ground as a young man in jogging pants rushed to her aid, knelt over her and gently patted her hand.

Matthew watched in a kind of daze as the man pulled out his cell phone to call for help. The young Asian mother he had observed earlier ran frantically from one person to the next desperately begging for assistance in what Matthew could only presume was her native tongue.

It was a language no one else seemed to speak, but Matthew's heart understood the high-pitched foreign babble falling from the woman's mouth at lightning speed.

He understood the bloodless pallor of her face and the utter despair and terror in her eyes clearly conveying the universal language of horror and loss, a language every loving parent speaks fluently.

"Dear God, help, me! My child is lost! Have you seen my baby? Where is my baby?" is what every fiber of the woman's being was screaming.

Yes, Matthew knew exactly what she was saying, and it no longer mattered where she came from or in what language she was saying it. He knew her baby was gone. His baby was gone, too, as were the children of everyone else in the park.

His head suddenly felt as though it was stuffed with cotton, and the ground came flying up toward him. The shock of it caused his legs to give way beneath him. He hit the ground hard and there he lay on his side, curled up like some wounded beast.

In that moment, a part of his soul died, as he became aware of the unspoken, often undetected connection a being has with its offspring had been abruptly severed. In that moment, Matthew Knightly knew his daughter Maia was no longer alive in the world. But it happened over three years and two weeks ago.

He thought he would have been compelled to keep track of the exact number of days, hours, and minutes that had passed since her disappearance. But he hadn't and therefore, he didn't. All he knew was he and a couple of billion other people on the planet became what the world's medical community politely called "A Patient Zero."

Together, they each learned the bottom line of their circumstance, which was "gone" was still "gone," and no matter how you counted, it would drive you even crazier than you had already become.

Not to mention that he honestly could not work out the logic of how well over a billion people could all be given the designation of Patient Zero. Three years ago, the patient number designation thing hadn't made any sense to him. But three years and one week later, it had begun to make more sense than he cared to think about. It meant he was no longer expected to be a rational, contributing member of society because of his Patient Zero status. And he was happy to oblige.

Even if a vast number of those with whom he'd had the "honor" of sharing the designation, were, according to the government "far less capable of coping on a daily basis and no longer the kind of people others wouldn't normally mind being associated with under different circumstances." Whatever the hell that meant. Things weren't normal anymore.

And nothing would ever be normal again, because God was real, and because exactly three years, two weeks, six hours, and twenty-two minutes ago, He had taken away Maia and every other child on the planet under the age of thirteen. All that remained of Matthew's soul following his introduction to "The One True God," amounted to less than the dusty millings of chalk from a blackboard left dancing amongst the last golden rays of sunlight on a lazy afternoon in June, moments before they were carried away on a breeze from an open schoolroom window, left ajar for just such a purpose.

So, Matthew decided he would do everything in his power to find this unquestionable God. And although it would probably be the last thing he ever did in his life, when he did find God (and he would find Him), he fully intended to kick the tyrant deity squarely in His lofty throat! An egomaniacal, insane, master plan? Perhaps. But hey, it was better than doing nothing. Right?

He used to think perhaps he should be a tad more concerned about the fact that his burning lust for revenge against God didn't scare him in the least. And the truth was it really didn't. It didn't scare him, at all. He had unmercifully lived through his worst nightmare, and the hopes of facing off with the Almighty and kicking His "holy" ass allowed Matthew to sleep perfectly well at night and gave him a reason to keep breathing the next day.

He had been mulling the same thoughts of revenge over in his mind for a little more than three years now, and he hadn't been struck down yet. So far, so good, right? Right.

And on each day during those three plus years, he had somehow managed to press the mute button on the nagging, tinny sounding voice he assumed was what was left of his shredded mental state. The voice that insisted on reminding him that he had absolutely no idea where to begin looking for Maia or the tyrant God that had snatched her away.

Matthew's horrific reverie began to fade, and the night sky started its steady trek high above the expanse of the Chicago skyline, bringing a cool breeze from one of the far reaches of Lake Michigan along with it. The dark jagged scar running a good four and a half inches down the right side of Matthew's face started to throb and sting. It was a familiar discomfort that told him two things as he absentmindedly ran his fingers along the length of the soft indentation marring his face.

The first being that the temperature was dropping, and the second was the realization that three years and two weeks ago might just as well have been three hours and two minutes ago. Maia's mother had given him the scar on the day their daughter vanished while in her father's care. While in *his* care. Every day. Every ... single ... day ... the scar would begin to sting whenever the temperature started to fall, which was usually in the evening.

And for those few excruciating minutes, it felt to Matthew as though his face had been slashed only seconds before. The pain was such that, at times, he expected his fingertips to feel the hot stickiness of fresh blood gushing from the wound like a punctured water hose. He could still see the faces of the two police officers who had driven him back to the modest two-story brick home Maia and her mother, Monica, shared with a four-legged ruddy-colored tuft of fur Maia had named "Tia."

Matthew often fought in the streets growing up, and occasionally with his own mother's worthless family members from time to time.

His mother's sister was an addict who had actually pulled a gun on him once after he refused to surrender the lunch money his mother had given him for school. There were very few things that unnerved him or made him fearful, but he was more than a little afraid of facing Monica that afternoon.

He had been riding in the back of a police car with two stoic looking officers he'd managed to flag down in the park. He told them someone had snatched his daughter. Yes. He had actually used the word "snatched," which, of course, turned out to be entirely true, even if he hadn't known it at the time.

The officers listened in complete disbelief, and were duly shuttling him into the back of their cruiser when they suddenly noticed a mass of people all screaming incoherently and running frantically in their direction. Something about the way the officers handled him let Matthew know they also realized that if they gave the crowd an opportunity to reach the cruiser, all three of them were going to find themselves trapped in the same boat, badge or no badge. But it wasn't until after the cruiser pulled out of the park rather too quickly and a bit recklessly from the gathering crowd that Matthew realized he was considered the lesser end of a far bigger and potentially much more dangerous problem.

After all, the pair was just supposed to be monitoring the park for the odd grouping of unruly teenagers, not suppressing a frantic mob of frightened parents.

And after listening in silent disbelief to the stream of panicked chatter on the police scanner about kids all over the city disappearing into thin air, it wasn't long before all three of them were on the verge of becoming unhinged.

That is … if what they were hearing on the scanner was to be believed. And they did believe it. God knew they didn't want to, but nevertheless they did.

The three of them sat in the cruiser riding through the city streets in stark, almost palpable silence. Each of them trying their damnedest not to think about what had supposedly happened in April 2023 and then once more the following April in 2024, when men, women, and children alike, all over the world supposedly had the same vision, or dream, or whatever one chose to call it. But whatever "it" was, "it" happened to everyone on the same night. Everyone described seeing the same light and hearing the same message coming from a voice speaking to them in their native tongue.

At that moment, however, neither Matthew nor the officers wanted to think about the fact that they, too, had experienced both dreams just like everyone else. Not now anyway, not today.

Besides, it was three years ago, and governments the world over said it was nothing more than an elaborate hoax put on by some eccentric bazillionaire who managed to privately launch a few dozen satellites in the middle of the night during the mid-2000s. He pulled it off by hacking into the signals of major cell phone and cable network carriers, and it had something to do with the new cell towers he had recently funded, or something like that.

Of course, no one bothered to explain away the case of the Sentinelese, a completely isolated indigenous people who inhabited a small island in the Bay of Bengal in India. They were so isolated, in fact, that their language was completely unknown to modern linguists. They were murderously hostile toward anyone from the outside world and had been so since at least the late 1700s.

But everything changed the day after the first "hoax" in 2023, when just after daybreak, a group of these reclusive, murderous little fellows canoed on over to the nearest shore, grinning from ear to ear, jabbering away, waving, and giggling like a bunch of silly school children at the local fishermen.

Of course, their gestures scared the locals half to death and sent them screaming into the streets and temples begging any holy man they could find for guidance in saving their lives.

They were only too glad to admit they had also dreamed the night before. It would later be discovered – after many long hours of giggling and drawing pictures in the sand – the Sentinelese had also managed to be manipulated by their dreams of the previous night. Like the rest of the world, each one had been instructed in their dream not to tell a living soul the specifics of what was said to them. What was said to them was meant for them and them alone. And they were to trust and do as the voice instructed.

All of this happened despite the Sentinelese never having any prior contact with the outside world, and never using a cell phone or watching television. They had never been near a cell tower, nor had any of them had so much as a tooth filling for that matter.

Matthew had a nasty urge to ask one of the officers what the date was, but as soon as he thought about it, he felt like someone had nailed his tongue to the bottom of his mouth. And for some reason he couldn't explain, he didn't exactly think it was a bad thing. At any rate, neither officer said a word after verifying Monica's home address with him, nor did they respond directly to anything that came across on the cruiser radio. Matthew didn't blame them. The trio continued in silence, only occasionally glancing nervously at one another, as they tried in vain to mask their own panic and confusion.

Matthew would only have a cursory memory of what was happening outside of the confines of the patrol car during the seemingly endless ride. He had been staring at his own hands, for the most part, and feeling like a man who knew he had left something important behind. Only he knew exactly what he had left behind, and the agony of not knowing where to begin looking for it had already started to eat away at what was left of his sanity. He had a vague sense of people in the streets yelling and crying and intermittently banging on the windows of the police cruiser whenever they stopped for a traffic signal.

After a while, one of the officers switched on the siren – traffic lights be damned. Matthew's guts had long since gathered into several knots back in the park, and the closer they got to their destination the harder his stomach started to cramp. He was surprised when neither of the cops suggested he might possibly have something to do with Maia being taken, or perhaps he knew something about why the other kids in the park had gone missing. Because well, Chicago cops just did not go around accusing people of crazy shit like that ... ever. If they had a man in their sights for spitting a wad of gum on the sidewalk, you had better believe the man was going to be questioned about three or four other crimes he didn't know a damn thing about, let alone had anything to do with.

When the patrol car finally pulled up in front of Monica's house, he and the officers approached the front door. Matthew had runnels of sweat streaming down his back and his hands started to shake. Even though he and Monica had never gotten around to getting married, she and Maia were still at the core of who he was and the focal point of the man he hoped to become one day. His fear of the repercussions of disappointing or hurting his daughter's mother far outweighed any fears he had of any God. And as it turned out ... his apprehensions were well placed.

Monica must have been waiting somewhere near the door; she answered the door too quickly.

Matthew's hands were shaking and sweating so badly he had barely pulled the house keys from his pant's pocket when she swung the door open so violently that he was nearly sucked into the front room, where a wall of sound from the television hit him squarely in the face. No doubt she had already received several frantic phone calls from her friends and family. She had been listening to the news while anxiously watching for anyone approaching the house.

The volume on the television was turned unnecessarily high, or maybe just high enough to drown out the desperate thoughts of a frantic parent. The emergency broadcast system alarm was blaring, while a soulless, mechanical voice, void of any human emotion recited a litany of "missing" children's names.

In the moment it took for Monica to open the door, Matthew and the officers glanced at the television screen and then at one another, each knowing it was a lie. None of those children were "missing." They were "gone."

Matthew absent-mindedly wondered how long the madness had been going on. An hour? Three hours? How long? How could the authorities already have a list of names? Where was the always-camera-ready, nonplussed, over-powdered human newscaster who was always on hand to announce the latest misery of Mankind to the world? Where were the videotaped reports and live, up-to-the-moment interviews of people on the streets to whom this nightmare was not happening? The realization of what the answer to these questions might mean made Matthew's intestines constrict.

Upon seeing Matthew with the officers and that Maia was not with them, and perhaps realizing her own baby's name would soon be added to the mechanical diatribe, the mother of Matthew's only child proceeded to lose her mind.

She buckled before anyone could catch her, sliding down the doorframe to her knees shrieking and clawing at her face and hair with both hands. A tortured wail rose from her throat and ended in a long bellowing "Nooooo!" loud enough to make the men turn their heads in pain with the shame of having returned empty-handed.

Neither Matthew nor the officers made any attempt to stop her from pushing past them and running toward the squad car. She screamed Maia's name and yanked frantically at the rear door handle of the sedan, but it was locked. She cupped her hands just above her eyes and pressed her tearstained face against the tinted windows in a desperate, but ultimately futile search for her child.

Matthew did not remember how Monica managed to close the distance between them as fast as she did, because she was not a small woman. But he would never forget what he saw when she turned back around to face them. Spittle dribbled unchecked from one corner of her mouth, and her wide, tortured frightened eyes full of longing and fear distorted her face.

He barely recognized her. But when her sunken eyes fixed their gaze upon him, his breath hitched and caught like a rock in his throat. And then she raged.

Monica screamed before anyone had time to react, a deep, guttural, primal scream. She charged at Matthew with her teeth bared in a wild, scratching fury of anger.

No one noticed the small, metal picture frame containing an image of Maia she was holding in the palm of her hand. Matthew liked to think perhaps in her moment of grief and anguish that Monica had forgotten she had it in her hand. Yes, he liked to think this was the case.

He felt nothing when she sliced the side of his face open. He remembered seeing the blood splatter across her face and feeling a warm, heavy wetness running down his neck and shirt collar. He hadn't even thought to raise his hands in self-defense. Perhaps, because even then, he knew he was to blame for awakening the wild-eyed, screeching thing that was being pulled off him by two police officers.

It wasn't until he registered the officers were attempting to restrain the woman who had given birth to his only child that he moved. He moved despite the stern rebukes from the officers and Monica's wailing and wild attempts to break free from their grasp. Matthew lovingly cupped Monica's face in his bloody hands and looked into her eyes.

When he saw they were empty, he embraced what of her he could, given that the police still held her. Her body went limp, the officers released their hold on her, and she fell sobbing into Matthew's arms.

Her strength spent, Matthew enfolded what was left of her rage and anguish into his arms and melded the slow death rattle of her soul with that of his own.

They had taken only two faltering steps before her legs buckled and her body crumpled like a marionette whose master had suddenly cut its strings. An almost inhuman, preternatural moaning rose from somewhere deep in her chest.

It was a sound that could only be described as a distorted cross between the cooing of a dove and the guttural growl of a nameless beast.

Matthew could feel her torso vibrating, and every instinct he had told him to let her go and back away. The sound turned his spine into a pole of ice, and he could feel the goose bumps running down his arms as if they were running for their lives. But, still, he held onto her – until he felt terror grip him unlike any fear he had ever felt before. A primal, dreadful knowing pulled at his bowels and brought him close to soiling himself. He knew if Monica were to evaporate as Maia had while he was holding her, his mind would become a twisted blackened rope of putrefied taffy. His psyche would be nothing more than a wet bog of insanity from which he could never emerge.

"Please God, no!" was Matthew Knighton's last audible plea to the sadist God – three years, two weeks, and nine days ago. The two officers offered their assistance in getting Monica back into the house, but the rising cacophony from the patrol car radio caught their attention and they simultaneously slowed their pace. Matthew looked at them and saw their fear-stricken faces for the first time, as the taller and he thought perhaps the younger of the two, was hard-pressed to tear his attention away from the patrol car.

Matthew imagined he could hear the man's brain clicking away behind his tawny eyes as he processed the heavily coded police chatter as swiftly as any seasoned secretary could convert spoken word into a legible form of modern-day hieroglyphics. What for the most part was an endless stream of number-coded gibberish to the untrained ear was apparently unsettling enough to drain the blood from the officer's face. The younger man turned to his partner and addressed the elephant in the room, the fear in his voice no longer in check, "Wallace, what in the hell is going on? Is this for real?"

But Wallace didn't have time to respond before the younger man sprinted back to the patrol car and got into the driver's seat.

He began mumbling utterances of disbelief to himself as he punched information into the iPad mounted on the dash next to the radio. When he saw his partner using the iPad, Wallace's blood ran cold. Perhaps because he hadn't been quite ready to let go of the notion that at any moment the little prick would turn and flash one of his stupid grins – just before fessing up to his part in making Wallace the butt of yet another one of his humorless jokes, one that would most likely cause a lesser man to go into cardiac arrest.

Or maybe, and he liked this idea better, he was still asleep, like he was last time and if so, it would be awfully nice if his wife, Ethyl, would just get on with jabbing her feet into the small of his back and nudging him so he could wake the fuck up already!

Waking up to his wife's ice-cold feet on his back had been more reliable over the last twenty years than any alarm clock and much cheaper than electric shock therapy.

But he didn't like where this particular dream was going, and it had been going full-speed ahead for quite some time now. Kinda like the last time, only this was worse.

The last time, it was just him and The Lord, and he had been safely tucked in his bed next to his Ethyl and her size ten ice packs. But now, well … now this was really happening. Wasn't it?

Wallace remained silent as he assisted Matthew in getting Monica back into the house and settled on the living room couch. He found the television remote and muted it so as not to further agitate the distraught woman. He remained with her while Matthew went into the kitchen to get a roll of paper towels to curb the bleeding on his face.

"Thanks, officer, I think I can manage from here," Matthew said wearily, perplexed as to why his own voice sounded funny to him, as if he had cotton stuffed in his ears. He could still hear the subterranean noise coming from Monica's throat, and it made him shudder.

"Wait," the sound of her voice startled them both, but Matthew was relieved she was no longer unconscious.

"You need a picture, right? A picture of my baby so you'll know her when you find her?" her voice cracked like the final croak of a dying toad, and when she lifted her head, her round, wet eyes silently pleaded with the officer to confirm her speculation.

"Yes, Ma'am, that might help things along." Wallace spoke to her quietly and carefully in the manner reserved for those whose loved ones were most likely already dead. But Monica didn't know that, so she rose from the couch with newfound purpose and disappeared down the narrow hallway just off the living room.

"She got you pretty good; you should have it stitched up. We can get the paramedics over here if you want. It might be easier for both of you if they gave her a sedative or something," Wallace said, pointing his head toward the hallway.

Matthew figured the officer had only offered to call an ambulance because it was protocol. Neither one of them wanted to admit they knew damn well that if he did make the call, no one would answer it. No one would be available to answer it. Not today anyway, and most likely not tomorrow, either. Because they would all be looking for their children, or their grandchildren, or their neighbor's children or, as Matthew was beginning to think, any children, at all.

Wallace's partner stopped short of coming into the house. He stood in the front doorway, breathing heavily with panic and sweating profusely. His eyes were round and wide with fear, and the smell of his fear wafted off him and into the house.

"Come on, we have to go! I need to get over to the school and get my kids! You won't believe the shit they're saying on the horn! I gotta go get my kids!"

He was pleading like a little boy who was begging his older brother to go down into the cellar with him to fetch whatever it was their mother wanted.

Then, he dashed back out the door toward the police cruiser that was beginning to draw a furtive crowd of men and women from the surrounding houses. Cries of "Excuse me, officer!" began to be heard up and down the block.

Wallace grimaced and sucked the air through his clenched teeth just like the older brother he intrinsically was, which was why he grew up to become an older brother to the people of an entire city. Even as his hopes that the strange events of the day would somehow manage not to get up close and personal were summarily dashed, Monica emerged from the hallway, clutching a five-by-seven picture of Maia to her breast.

"Here, this is my Maia. She's five years old and she's wearing this same outfit today ... it's her favorite," her voice trailed off, perhaps realizing she sounded mechanical, like one of those robot women from the movie *The Stepford Wives*.

Monica handed the photo over to Wallace, never once taking her eyes off the picture as she relinquished it. Nor did she appear to notice the bloody thumbprint she left on the narrow silver border of the photograph. For a flickering moment, Matthew thought she just might snatch the picture back and hold it one last time.

But the moment passed, and the corner of her mouth twitched impulsively as she murmured what might have been a feeble "thank you."

She sat back down on the couch and turned toward the television and watched in silence as random images of missing children began to parade across the screen.

Then, both men saw something that made their breath hitch and their blood run cold. The chyron ribbon running across the bottom of the television screen read: April 29, 2027 – Children Reported Missing Worldwide

"You have kids?" Matthew asked the officer in a voice that was barely audible. Wallace's gaze went from the back of Monica's head to the television screen and the countless young faces systematically flashing like a set of slides in one of those old round Kodak projectors from the 1970s.

There was fear in his eyes as he watched the images in silence, because they somehow made things seem even more unsettling – if this was even possible – and the older man shuddered before he answered Matthew.

"No. No, I don't. But it don't make it no easier." His voice came out in a hushed whisper, in case someone was listening. *Hell*, he thought. *Maybe the poor woman was right to crank the volume up, after all.*

2

Standing on the Fingertip of God

"**C**ome on! Come on! Pick up!" Danny yelled, holding onto the telephone receiver with a vice-like grip while frantically pacing the floor of his tiny studio apartment like a caged animal. He released the phone and used his shoulder to hold it against his right ear as he pulled a cell phone out of his pants pocket and started to search through the recent call listings on the tiny LED screen. He was looking for Herman's number and inwardly cursed himself for never having gotten around to putting the cameraman's number on speed dial. "Why wasn't his number on speed dial? And why the wasn't Chima answering the goddamn phone?"

As if in answer to his mental query, he finally heard the tinny ringing on the other end of the line replaced with the distinct clang of someone fumbling to answer before dropping the receiver on what Danny could only guess was the floor. The clang sounded exactly like what he imagined a gunshot would sound like if a .45 caliber were discharged in his head. "Shit!" he screamed as the phone fell off his shoulder and into his fumbling hands. He quickly recovered and put the receiver back up to his ear.

"Chima? Chima, it's Danny. I need you to get your ass out of bed and meet me over at the pad in fifteen! Chima?"

A groggy and perturbed voice mumbled what he could only guess was the equivalent of "Why? What is it?"

"There's a jumper on The Redeemer and no one's got it yet. So, get your ass outta bed and be at the helio pad in ten! I'm calling Herman now!" He hung up the landline receiver and replaced it with the cell phone, which had rung no more than twice on the other end before it was picked up.

"Herman, we've got a hot one. Pack up your gear and get your ass over here, now! Yes, I know what time it is – what's your point? That's what I thought. See you in ten," Danny abruptly disconnected the call.

"Was that the phone?" said Sarala Chima, peeking her head around the doorframe of her daughter's bedroom.

"Yeah. It's nothing, Mommy. Just an early shoot for Danny, but I gotta go." Anit Chima's thick, black hair was bunched into a frazzled topknot. She sat up on the edge of her bed and gently rubbed the sleep from her eyes.

"But it's still dark outside! How can you do anything at this time of the morning? It's only a little after three," Sarala's eyes were wide with maternal concern for her thirty-two-year-old baby. Anit shot her mother a look they were both well acquainted with, and Sarala shrugged her shoulders to concede the point as she tightened the belt of her housecoat.

"I'll make you some coffee then," she said, which was more or less her way of saying, "Well, you can't stop me from at least doing that."

"Thanks Mommy, but make it quick. Danny's already having a fit."

"When isn't Danny having a fit?" Sarala shot back before exiting the room. She closed the door firmly behind her, which was another way of ensuring she had the last word on the subject. Anit rose to her feet and bounded into the bathroom. She rinsed off in a ten-second cold shower, and within the next five minutes she was standing at the front door with her burly knapsack slung over one shoulder and a thermos full of hot black coffee in her hand.

"That's yesterday's joe. I figured you didn't have time to wait for it fresh," her mother cautioned. Anit planted a kiss on her mother's cheek. "You figured right. Thanks, Mommy. Love you, bye."

"Be careful." Sarala said this last comment to her herself because by then Anit was already down the stairwell and out the door. She listened as her daughter's Wrangler pulled out and rumbled loudly down the hill of their narrow street in first gear, before skidding around the corner. Sharala groggily made her way back into their modest kitchen to brew a fresh pot of coffee for herself. She had a nagging suspicion she wouldn't be going back to sleep anytime soon.

Fifteen minutes later, Anit rounded a deserted street corner and brought her Jeep to a full stop just outside the helipad parking lot.

The electronic chain link fence was closed and locked; she entered an access code and took her pick of the empty parking spaces that lay beyond the gate. As she walked across the tarmac toward the dark chopper, she could see two men standing nearby in the shadows. Both were smoking and one was pacing back and forth like a restless tiger while yelling at some poor soul on the other end of his cell phone. It was her boss, Danny Garcia.

"No! Don't you dare call the cops! All I need is ten minutes. Victor, we're family and you owe me! Yeah, yeah, I swear. Whatever, man, look … ten minutes and then you can call in the National Guard if you want. All I'm asking for is a head start, alright? Okay. Thanks." Danny hung up the phone and turned his attention and his agitation directly at Anit.

"Goddamnit, Chima, I said ten minutes! What took you so long?"

She looked at him dryly with hooded eyes and an expression that clearly said she could care less about his timetable.

"Don't swear at me! You said fifteen minutes! And I'm here now, so give it a rest."

She turned and gave a broad smile and friendly greeting to the tall, lanky man standing nearby. "Hey, Hermie!"

Herman nodded his head in silence and picked his gear up off the ground, all the while holding a lit cigarette tightly between his lips. She liked Herman; he only spoke when it was necessary, and he rarely found it necessary.

"You know the rules; put those things out before getting in my bird," Anit said, casually chastising them as she unlocked the cabin of the helicopter and tossed her flight pack behind the pilot's seat. She was pleased with her decision to buy the new insulated flight suit she wearing because the air was rather cold this time of morning, even for Brazil. It would be even colder once they were airborne. She climbed into the pilot's seat and once strapped in, she started the rotor blades and felt the familiar, ready to rock n' roll tap on her left shoulder from Herman.

Danny was still bitching about the time as she flipped the many switches and knobs required to bring the metal bird to life.

Anit grabbed a couple of headpieces from their storage compartments and casually tossed them to the men. Within a matter of seconds, Danny was chattering away in her ear like a rabid squirrel, rattling off meaningless instructions as she expertly guided the helicopter off the ground and into the night sky.

It was a familiar routine. Anit punched in a flight plan and saw to other important duties necessary to keep the bird aloft. Herman readied his camera equipment in silence, and Danny continued speaking to no one in particular in his rapid-fire, barking manner. Neither she nor Herman acknowledged a word he said. No one listened to Danny Garcia unless it was necessary.

With a long drawn-out sigh of resignation, Anit reluctantly submitted to the necessity.

"Alright boss, what gives? All I know is we're headed for The Redeemer," she asked.

"Goddamnit, Chima – get your head in the game! There's a jumper and we've got first dibs. That is, we will if you can get this tin can over there in ten."

"Why is everything 'in ten' with you?" Herman chimed in over the headphones. Anit knew Herman could care less about an answer to his question. The man was a wiz with a camera and a loner by anyone's standards. His question to Danny was his feeble attempt at "involvement."

"Shut it!" Danny anxiously reprimanded them both. "Listen, my cousin works security over there, and he says there's a jumper. He called me because he thought it would make a decent scoop."

"What about the police? We might have a problem flying over in the middle of a rescue."

"There are no police. Not yet anyway. Like I said, I was the first call he made."

"That's not what you said. And you told him not to call for some real help? What if the guy jumps?" Anit feigned concern and shock. In truth, she wasn't shocked, at all, but she figured it would look better in court if and when they nailed Danny's ass for involuntary manslaughter.

"My cousin agreed to give us a ten-minute head start before calling the cops, that's all. For once, I'd like for us to get a story before people start taking pictures on their phones and selling them to TMZ."

"Hermie, you cool with this?" Anit's voice fully suggested she was hoping he was not.

"I'm cool with a paycheck," Herman replied flatly, as he casually gazed out the starboard window.

"Kick this thing in gear, will you? By the time we get there, the frikkin' National Guard will already be there!"

"Keep your panties on. There he is." Anit's voice came out in a whisper filled with reverence, as it always was whenever she approached the iconic statue. But something about this visit was different, perhaps because there was a super moon looming heavily in the night sky right behind the stone monument.

Normally, the monument is a sight that can stir the soul of any man, woman, or child who is fortunate enough to bear witness to it. She approached the statue from the East as she always did, because something about flying in the face of God unnerved her, even if it was just a statue. And there he was, Christ The Redeemer, in all his glory, standing with both arms outstretched on the top of a mountain with the fullness of a dusty yellow super moon swallowing up the sky behind him. It was more than a humbling sight; it was enough to drive the faithful prostrate.

The two-hundred-foot-tall behemoth was swathed in the light of a moon bright enough to drown out the high beams from the two dozen or so halogen lights embedded in the circular concrete base upon which it stood. As if this visage was not enough of a shock to the senses, on the outstretched right arm of the statue, nearest the wrist, stood the distinct form of a human figure.

"Holy, shit!" Danny's voice was a harsh croak in Anit's headset, and it sounded a lot like he was trying to hold back a scream. The figure had their back to them, and as they flew in closer, they could see it was a woman dressed in a long white gown, not unlike the long, cotton nightshirts those Victorian-era characters wore in just about every Jane Austin movie Anit had ever seen.

"Get your cousin on the phone and tell him to call the police, Danny. Now!" she scolded him harshly. She wanted nothing to do with whatever this crazy person had in mind. It wasn't just the girl she was thinking about either; everyone knew Danny Garcia was as crazy as a loon when it came to scoring a scoop. There wasn't much he wouldn't at least think about doing in the name of a good story.

"Fuck that, my cousin is an idiot. I'll call," he retorted, surprising both Anit and himself.

Anit held the bird as steady as she could, all the while staring in disbelief at the svelte, young woman standing on the thumb of the statue.

She cocked her head to one side, trying to recall the moment when the woman had moved from the statue's wrist over to the thumb. And how had she done it? It was anyone's guess as to the actual width of the space where she was now standing. The depth of the blackness that lay below the woman's current perch made Anit's skin crawl.

But there she stood. A young woman, no more than a waif really, standing motionless with her back to them. Her long, brown, wavy hair fell in a wide cascade over her shoulders and down to the middle of her narrow back.

"The cops are on the way," Danny murmured. "Jesus, how'd she get up there? Herman, are you getting this? I want some shots from the front. Chima, can you get in front of her?"

"The draft from the rotors might blow her off if I try to do anything except back up," Anit explained without taking her eyes off the woman. Out the corner of her eye she could see Herman moving in closer with his camera lens.

"Hang on, what's that? Is it blood?" Danny was leaning toward the windshield of the bird with his nose almost touching the glass.

Anit followed his gaze toward the girl's feet and she, too, could see there was indeed blood dripping ... no gushing, from the soles of the girl's feet down and over the sides of the concrete where she stood.

"That's not possible. How is so much blood possible?" Anit murmured to herself as the torrent of blood from the girl's feet flowed onto the statue's hand.

"Holy Mother of God." Herman's voice came from the rear of the helicopter in a hoarse and haunted whisper. What happened next would randomly replay itself in Anit's mind for the remainder of her days. The moment those words were uttered, the girl turned completely around as though she had heard Herman speak from inside the helicopter.

Despite the thick Plexiglas windshield separating its occupants from the outside world, the sound of the wind and the whirling of the helicopter rotors, she moved as effortlessly as if she were standing in the center of a grand ballroom rather than a two-foot-wide precipice atop the forefinger of a statue standing more than two hundred feet in the air.

Anit clearly heard Herman's breath catch in his chest like a rabbit caught in a snare. The woman's soft, almond-shaped, hazel brown eyes looked right into their stunned faces and they could plainly see she couldn't have been more than seventeen years old.

But, in the next instant, her serene features appeared to morph ever so slightly, until there was something about her that could make one believe she might have been as old as twenty-five. Anit was hard pressed to grasp anything she couldn't rationalize into existence.

Her mind was so analytical that the concept of secondhand smoke had been difficult for her to swallow. She had never seriously contemplated the existence of supernatural beings, but she knew instinctively the young woman standing on the fingertip of Christ The Redeemer was as calm as if she were standing in the middle of a football stadium, and she was surely made of something far sturdier than the rest of Mankind.

Anit was about suggest she maneuver the helicopter away from the statue when the buffoon she referred to as her "boss" uttered a profanity in God's name. And in the blink of an eye, the woman's large brown, doe-like eyes looked directly at Danny as the three of them stared back at her, mesmerized with terror. The flushed lips of the young woman's delicate mouth never moved, and even if they had, there would be no way for them to hear the words she uttered. Anit knew that look, though. She had witnessed it countless times in the eyes of her own mother. It was the look that said, "Come now. You know better." What child didn't recognize such a gaze?

Hector would swear on the life of his precious mother that there had been an audible gasp within the confines of the cockpit, despite the whirring of the rotor blades and the headphone he wore over one ear. Up until that moment, Hector had loved his mother more than any other being known to him, including God. But when the young woman's eyes pivoted to gaze upon his face, and he fully looked at her calm, dovelike features, his heart had room for no other. Her face emanated a soft glow that seemed to come from within. To say the young woman standing before them was beautiful would have been a gross overstatement.

She was olive-skinned with smooth but indistinguishable features, making it impossible to say what race or creed of people could claim her. Her face was perfectly framed by a long frothy mass of dark brown curly hair. Her nose was slightly wider than expected on such a face wrought with Anglo, Negroid, and Asiatic features all at once. They watched as her features continued to shift ever so slightly, making her face appear to resemble every semblance of Mankind, but not anyone in particular. The flowing eggshell-colored garment she wore was actually a long tunic made from a light woven wool or linen cloth. And the three of them could plainly see the front of the garment was heavily bloodstained in the area just below the woman's pubis.

The blood coming from the sacred and secret place between her legs ran like water down her covered legs, between and over her bare feet, pooling in the hem of her garment before dripping freely onto the surface of the statue. Anit heard her companions moan in despair, and she herself felt her heart swell with a sudden and inexplicable sense of sorrow. She felt as though her very soul wanted to burst free from its fleshy cage.

Even Danny was shamed by the sight, and he whimpered ever so softly at his inability to avert his eyes in an effort to un-see what his mind knew to be true.

Anit saw it too – saw the unreal visage of a girl who was obviously menstruating, but her rational mind screamed it could not be happening. The blood was literally gushing from beneath the bloodstained garment, over the girl's bare feet and onto and over the edges of the hand of the statue upon which she stood. It didn't take much for Anit to imagine that if she had approached the statue from the front, facing its open palms, it would look much the same way it might have when the edifice's namesake was nailed to a piece of wood more than three thousand years ago. The thought made her blood turn to ice. She tried in vain to calculate how much blood it would take to create such a sight, knowing instinctively that no human body contained such an amount. And even if it could, it would have been impossible for this girl to remain standing after losing so much of it.

Yet, there she stood, and the blood continued to gush forth in a veritable torrent. Anit was able to tear her gaze away long enough to witness the streams of blood falling from the statue's hand before getting caught up in the high winds created by her rotors and disappearing somewhere in the blackness below.

Danny uttered the name of "Jesus" and they watched as a slow pleasing smile moved across the pale rose-colored lips of the girl, as if she had heard Danny speak.

The girl then took one step outward into the vast darkness below, and Hector screamed the name of God.

But before the scream Anit was working on could leave her throat, the woman suddenly appeared standing on the nose of the helicopter with her face less than three feet away from them. She had somehow crossed the wide void of space between the aircraft and the statue, as if she were simply stepping from one spot to another. Time seemed to stop. The young girl stood on the nose of the aircraft with a serene smile and simply looked directly at Anit. There was a sound above the noise of the rotors, and Anit would later come to understand it had been the sound of Danny's high-pitched screams of sheer, unabashed terror. She would later remember seeing Herman out of the corner of her eye falling to his knees in prayer, desperately clutching a cross she had never noticed he wore on a gold chain around his neck.

But her eyes were transfixed on the girl's face, a face with olive skin, full, rounded cheekbones and a mouth that was smooth and soft, the color of a pale spring rose.

The young woman leaned in closer to the windshield, and the fear she would come right through the glass caused Anit to press her own body as far back into the pilot's seat as she could. The thick, tinny aroma of fresh blood flooded Anit's nostrils, making her head swim.

It was the smell of life, a scent only a woman knows and fully understands. It was the warm and sticky coppery smell of life and shame all rolled up into one.

But somehow, she knew there was no shame to be found in this young woman. Shame could never reside in such a one as she who stood before her.

"The blood returns," said the woman. Anit heard her dusky voice clearly and distinctly in her head – a calm, soothing and comforting voice as warm as a blanket that had wrapped itself around her entire being. As the thought passed through her mind, the girl nodded as if satisfied she had successfully related some unspoken message and Anit had finally understood. The young woman slowly raised her right hand and revealed her palm to them. It was empty save for a tiny ball of bright, golden light that began to swell from its center. Anit felt her breath hitch in her chest, and the light suddenly became too bright to look at directly.

Next, there was an abrupt flash, which momentarily blinded them all, and Anit raised one arm to her face and cried out in pain. And then came the sound Anit Chima had dreaded hearing all her life. It was a sound she had never heard before, but which had driven her to pursue a life of flight to abort her fear of it.

It was the terrifying crunching sound of something forcing its way down through the branches and limbs of heavy and healthy tree cover. It was the cracking sound of a windshield and the crunching and screeching sound made by metal folding in upon itself as it gave way to the unyielding hardness of the ground.

The last thing Anit saw was the bright flash of light and the image of the young girl's face as it burned into the fabric of her mind. Then, everything went black and was silent. Silent as a tomb ... silent as any grave.

3

The Arrival of the Arch Amun

A mun heard the voice of his creator cutting through his thoughts like a lightning strike with the added edge of a finely honed blade. The command had come fast and hard, a steady, pressing force of sheer will in his spirit.

"Now!" the voice had bellowed, although it was much more than a just a voice, and more than any sound or sensation a lower sentient creature was capable of comprehending. Every molecule comprising the being that was Amun, the Arch, every atom of his countenance had sparked and fired, pulsated, and jumped at the command of that which had willed him into existence. The Creator had spoken, and all that had been created in His shadow responded to the sound of His voice.

Amun allowed his thoughts to flow freely as he felt himself hurled through the folds of space and time toward the living sphere the Sons of Man called "Earth." So simple and beautiful it was from where he approached yet a dark sadness came to him when his thoughts turned toward the infestation upon her that was "Man." It had not always been so, but so it had become. Man's kind covered the skin of the planet like a pox. And he could see even from his great height that man's selfishness had begun to create an unending and possibly irreversible tumultuous clutter in the space surrounding the blue sphere.

The Creator had placed Mankind where it should want for nothing in His absence, and yet it was not enough. The planet had become laden with the presence of her charge. Full as a woman with child, she could keep herself no longer. Her semblance flexed, swollen, bleeding and cracked, her waters surging forth with the poison of man. Yet, few knew she had stopped breathing long ago. When her eye to God's infinity began to cloud and blur, she could hold herself no longer.

Terra had cried out to her Lord, saying, "It is time Father, for I can bear no more." And then she wept. Her water surged and her life's blood spewed from the mountains above and below her surface. She shuddered with quakes and her surface split into many pieces and in many places as she bled. The Earth heaved and the Lord caught her exhaled breath in his open palm and was vexed.

He had told the scourge that was "Man" this day would come, and they would one day crane their stiff necks to the sky and see the angels of God raining down upon them with their salvation in one hand and the sword of His vengeance in the other. He foretold the newly found arrogance of Man would not allow them to see or believe the Lord, their God, was once again among them. The day, unbeknownst to angel or Man had finally come. The call of God had come because of the cries of His daughter, the Earth, who had neither the strength nor the will to expel Mankind from her flesh.

But when Man dared to block the celestial light from her sight with his artificial veil of metal debris, she cried out in fear of no longer being able to see the face of God. It is all any daughter had to do – and now, this day, this night and seven more nights hence, my brethren and I shall descend upon the earth. We shall be the balm that soothes her tired, cracked, weary and poisoned flesh to rid her of the scourge that has tormented her for so long.

The Musings of Amun:

"I have no malice toward Man, for I was not created thusly. But you must know the pain of the foundation upon which he has so graciously been given and has so wantonly misused. You must understand her pain to accept Man's consequence in the matter. The Iyrin were not created with judgment; we were created for and with one purpose – to obey the will of our Creator.

"As I approached the atmosphere of Earth, I could feel the spirit flesh of my face getting warmer. Sweet Earth was covered in a warm blanket of clouds, but the festering wounds inflicted upon her within and without by Mankind smelled of rot. My task would be daunting, but I rejoiced at the thought of returning to the sphere, which simultaneously supported the pain and the beauty of life. There were worlds far older and some might say, far prettier, but none teemed with the variety of life and color that dwelt upon and within Earth. She was indeed the greenhouse of the universe."

Amun enjoyed this moment of mental freedom. He relished his dark thoughts of Mankind and the intense regard he felt for the planet Earth. His love was for the Earth as she had been before the blight that was Humankind and his many "creations," his unnecessary machines, and his poisons. Man's arrogance and innumerable dark experiments were conducted upon his own kind in a never-ending desire to stand as an equal with The Creator, and it was an appalling and extremely offensive thing to do.

These were his few dark and free thoughts concerning his utter disdain for and disappointment in Humankind. These forbidden judgments would be wiped from his spirit upon reaching the atmosphere. This was done to all his kind, for the burden that was the judgment of Man was not the place, nor the purpose of The Iyrin. Amun and his kind could neither love in excess nor hate any living thing upon the Earth while it rested upon the Earth.

He would exist in the moment of whatever his experience among Humankind would bring. He would act accordingly and to and for the purpose of which he had been created. Either to preserve life or extinguish it, without judgment, without hate, without sorrow and at times, without pity, regret, or remorse. These things came with the grace of free will and did not reside within the one who had been created with and for a sole purpose such as The Iyrin. In this moment, he could openly envy the free will of Man.

And yet the number of men who would ever know the true and full love of The Father could be counted by looking at a fixed point in the night sky. Considering there existed an ethos of stars in the heavens, this was saying little.

Amun smiled with joy in reaching the outer atmosphere of the Earth. He thought he would sense the others descending with him, but he did not. He did not think The Father would send him to Earth alone, but neither could he ever question the will of his Creator. His faith was his essence, and the faith The Father had in him to fulfill his purpose fueled what humans would call the "soul" of his kind. Yes, even The Iyrin, which Man would come to call "Angels" and "Beings of Light" have souls. It is the building block of The Creator.

Although the souls of angels had not been crafted in the same manner as those placed within the Beings of Dust, The Creator came to refer to Earth's humans as "Man." For the soul of a Man might choose to turn away from the face of God without regret for all eternity should he so desire. An act even the first of us was created, who in arrogance turned his back to our Father, could not do so without returning and bowing his head underneath the palm of The Creator's hand for permission to rule, even if it be in eternal shame and darkness.

Amun thought of how happy Man could be if only he could let go of his arrogance and insatiable lust for mortal flesh and God-like glory. How they would rejoice if they knew how an untethered soul soared across the endless heavens, free of the boundaries of the flesh. Unfortunately, this option had been taken away from Man, but this is another, albeit well known story. Man's arrogance allows him to find reason in glorifying his affronts to God. This was one of Amun's last thoughts before he entered the cluttered upper atmosphere of Earth.

The Arch, who only seconds before had rejoiced in his freedom to openly express disdain for Humankind, had one final and natural thought of sympathy and pity for that which he might soon be called upon to destroy. The unfamiliar, sour stench of what Humankind considered progress assaulted him as he passed through the Earth's stratosphere.

It was the reek of chaff and the remnants of unknown substances left over from centuries of long-forgotten experiments. The stink of destruction and decay perpetuated in the name of progress. And intermingled with it all was the malodor of the Earth herself, her sickness, her rot, was like the smell of someone near death. Amun shook the tears from his eyes. How like a man he was after all, for it was not the smell alone that made his tears come. But rather the deeply rooted pain he felt in his soul for the wounded Earth and every living thing abiding within and upon her.

And then he felt the reassuring hands of his Father rest firmly upon his shoulders. And in an instant, he was fortified, full of warmth and contentment, with a fiercely renewed sense of purpose. Amun's spirit was again in the throws of ecstasy, with the joy of having finally been chosen and called upon to serve.

The high, snow-covered peaks of the Earth spun below him as he traveled unseen across her face. At an immeasurable speed he approached the Tian Shan mountain range of the Asian continent, where it was night on this side of the world. Oh, how many eons by the clocks of Man had it been since he last touched this mountain face? By the light of the moon, and with eyes that could see all things by the dim light of the stars above, he made out and set his mind to the narrow passage that would take him to the sacred place he sought.

The place where he and others had walked in the shadow of The Creator some countless millennia long past, before man's footprint was upon the earth, there had been a temple where he and his brethren had toiled happily while their Father contemplated amongst the trees in his favorite garden. On those days not long forgotten, one could hear the humming of God.

4

Voices

Terris knew it was going to be cold, but jeezus, not this damn cold! But then again, any Black man who pulls a half-baked plan out of his ass to trek to the back end of beyond somewhere in the mountains of China–pretty much deserves whatever he gets. He'd always despised the cold, and now this is exactly what he was – cold! And it wasn't no punk-ass cold, either! Not like back in the states. No. This was "Bitch, you in the mountains of China now! And over here we do whatever the fuck we like!" kind of cold.

It was getting dark and the freezing winds traversing the landscape laughed at him quite murderously. It laughed at his age. It laughed at the color of his skin and mercilessly targeted his hairless head; despite the fact his head was currently swaddled beneath several layers of heavily woven woolen cloth and a shearling sheepskin hat. He had known it wasn't going to be enough, even as he bartered for the numerous hodgepodge ensembles of indigenous clothing, scarves, and pieces of clothing to wear underneath and over his western clothing. He hoped proper insulation would make the difference between the continuation of his life or subsequent death in the penetrating cold of the Asiatic mountains. For even now, his anticipation of the impending colder night ahead was beginning to grate on his mind.

His thoughts began to travel in circles, and for a few terrifying moments, he could not fathom who he was or how in the hell he had gotten to this forsaken place. But therein lies the story. How, and perhaps more importantly, why, a middle-aged Black man from Addison, Illinois was making his way through a remote mountain range in Asia alone and in the dead of winter, no less. The "how" of his circumstance was progressive; the "why," however, was the unfathomable part.

The whole venture up to this point had taken a little over a year to complete. Because not only was he uncertain as to exactly where he was going, he had absolutely no idea why he was trying to get there. All he knew was he had to be in these mountains at this particular time. Starving and cold as he was, he nonetheless had to be here. Somehow, he knew, in fact, that he was supposed to be here.

A biting, icy breeze unexpectedly hit an exposed portion of his cheek, and he instinctively tucked his head downward. In the same moment, his thoughts immediately went to the last hours he'd spent with his youngest sister, Athena. Why did cold make a man think? He remembered standing in the warmth of Athena's modest kitchen back in Chicago, working on his third cup of coffee at 10:30 on a Saturday morning. He habitually rose at 4:00 a.m. each day, but so as far as his body was concerned, it might as well have already been late afternoon.

The night before, he'd decided he should let at least one person know he was planning on leaving town for an extended period of time, even though it mattered little to him to also let said individual know he had no plans of ever coming back. Terris remembered briefly wondering morning if would be the last time he ever saw his baby sister.

The thought bruised his heart a bit more than he had anticipated, and so he settled for simply telling her that he would be "out of pocket" for a few weeks. In the end, they both knew whatever excuse he chose really didn't matter. Athena had always been smarter than most, and she knew he was purpose-fully misleading her.

Alright, yes ... it had been an outright lie, and they both knew it. But the one thing he had come to love and appreciate about his sister was the fact she always had the decency not to make an issue about such things as the truth between siblings. He could have said he was going to the moon for a few days, and the only message she would have taken from the conversation was that her brother would be unavailable for an unspecified period of time and she shouldn't worry about him. Anything more, she didn't need to know and he had no intention of telling her. He knew it and she knew it – and that was the end of it. But then, out of nowhere, she asked him if he loved her. Not meaning herself, but rather the woman Terris had been fairly sure (up until that point, at least) that his well- meaning sister knew nothing about.

He had been seeing a woman, one woman in particular as a matter of fact, for the better part of two years, and he hadn't mentioned her to anyone, not even Athena.

Terris was drinking his coffee and distinctly remembered stopping mid-sip and directing his infamous and pointed "back off" glare at her from over the rim of the cup, which was still raised to his lips. It was a look he hardly ever used on her, one that normally would have shut down any further lines of inquiry rather quickly. It usually resulted in the person on the receiving end making feeble attempts at fumbling through a string of apologies for crossing whatever invisible line Terris had suddenly thrown into the situation. But this was Athena, his favorite sister, and she was having none of it. She merely stood quietly, stared unfazed and frankly right back at him while waiting for an answer. Here he was, supposedly "Mr. Tough Guy," and his baby sister had called his bluff. She hadn't even blinked. *Damn*, he thought. *I'm getting old.*

He put his coffee cup down on the counter and gazed out of the front picture window of the house. For a moment, he imagined he was ten years old again, his mind busy plotting out the adventures to be had on the other side of the same glass. It was almost 1973 again, but in an instant the memory was gone.

"Well, do you?" Athena's tone told him she had dug her nails into the subject with no intention of releasing it without hearing a decent bit of "dirt," as they used to call it.

Thinking back on that morning, Terris knew full well he did indeed love the woman in question. He knew it. And looking back, he believed he had said as much to his sister.

The problem was ... he couldn't exactly remember thinking it or saying it. He couldn't remember actually forming the words, nor could he recall hearing himself say, "Yes, I do. I love her very much as a matter of fact."

He hated himself for not being sure of the moment. Had he said it? More importantly, had he ever told her – the woman in question – that he loved her? The woman whose name he could no longer bear to think about, let alone actually say it. The woman he had unceremoniously left 6,586 miles behind him without so much as a goodbye. Yes. He had loved her. A little too much.

His thought of "too much" got to him – that and the painful longing he felt for her, at times, which haunted and weakened him. He was not a young man, fifty-four to be exact, but he was a man who had come to know himself well. A man who had lived enough of his life to know not to allow his affections for any woman get the better of him. Although he had certainly enjoyed his fair share of relationships throughout the course of his life.

He was equally thankful he could count on one hand the number of times a woman had moved him to feel the way he now felt about her. The number was two. Both of which had culminated in marriage and ended in divorce. He had been emotionally eviscerated twice too many times because of his love for a woman who was disguised as a kitten. He had learned, by way of those two attempts, that once you allow a woman to curl up like a napping kitten in the warm, soft spot just underneath the base of your heart, you had no one else to blame when said kitten turns into a raging, claw-bearing, rabid hellcat who eats your guts for dinner!

He'd be damned if he'd find himself in that skillet a third time. So, he had kept "her" and his kryptonite at a physical and emotional distance.

In Terris' world, if you have lost your way in a forest, stop walking and get your bearings by finding which way is east. He knew this was a stupid and mannish way of thinking, but the metaphor was irrelevant to the situation. This was just how he saw it, and it was how he chose to see it. And so, like a pubescent teenager, he spent his days trying not to think about the woman he loved.

Terris' exterior completely belied the man he truly was on the inside, a middle-aged man who, in all honesty, didn't look a day over forty – a well-built, impeccably dressed and groomed individual whose hands were registered as lethal in no less than two states.

These same hands remained in high demand on numerous construction sites throughout the City of Chicago. His voice was a deep, unmistakable baritone that brought to one's mind the infamous science-fiction character once voiced by the actor James Earl Jones. His knowing smile or a harsh look of displeasure, coupled with the natural weightiness of his hands, spoke volumes to any who might oppose him. His manner was friendly or curt, as necessary, the necessity of which was, more often than not, dictated by the person with whom he was engaged. He liked to think of himself as a flowing river coursing through the terrain of life. But this was his illusion, a fictional self-assessment he shared with no one. The bottom line of which was he needed to feel in control of all factors in his life, even if maintaining control meant not being present or available to love or be loved, much less hurt.

He was barely fifteen when he learned the carpentry trade from an uncle. A year prior to his apprenticeship, he discovered he also had a profound love for the martial arts. These two skills would continue to develop throughout his life, and any novice philosopher worth his weight in salt would equate Terris with the living embodiment of the Chinese Yin and Yang. His trade-worn, heavily calloused hands were as equally capable of destruction as they were of creation. Although he was not a large man, not especially tall or overly broad, he possessed an undeniably formidable presence upon entering a room. Everything about him belied who he (and his mental and physical capabilities) really was. His half-century of life had taken more twists and turns than most. And no one, not even those he considered life-long or even particularly close friends, would ever know all he had witnessed or done. He was the alpha male in any room he entered and few other than the arrogantly foolish would argue that point.

Terris was a man with a purpose to survive. His survival had been for a task unspoken, unthought-of, and unclear for as long as he could, or rather could not remember. Yet, he had always lived with the knowledge, in fact, the surety, there was something he must do. Some "thing" that was not yet clear or fully focused. Not yet. Not yet – but soon – very soon.

Fifty-four years ago, he was born the second of nine children being raised in a volatile neighborhood on the West Side of Chicago. He was found to be smarter than most, a fast- thinking young man who made up for what he lacked in size with unbridled fearlessness and loyalty when it came to the childhood dealings of the inner-city youth.

It was a noble time, very much unlike the current state of the city. A time when all matters concerning those under the age of eighteen were settled fairly, albeit not always amicably, before the streetlamps came on in front of the two-story frame house where he, his three brothers, and five sisters shared four rooms with their parents. Terris learned at an early age the advantages the art of articulation could bring. He also quickly learned the challenges and insults it could incite in those who were supposed to be your friends.

It soon became clear these sworn, life-long alliances would only hold true so long as there was never any money involved, and he never attempted to think himself one iota better than the company he kept. But this is exactly what he thought and felt in his heart to be true whenever he was with anyone, no matter who it was. Except when he was with her, everyone ... except her. Immediately, he tried to force himself to think of something, anything, other than her. Anything! She had become his weakness, and he was in no way comfortable with it! But it was too late. She was here on this mountain, in his thoughts, and in his heart ... again.

There were times, not so odd as this one, when on some random mountainside in Asia he thought he could smell her ... a mixture of her light, musky sweat and the floral perfume she sometimes wore. It was a uniquely cloying scent that had oftentimes caused him to toy with the thought that perhaps she had it specially made somehow so only he could smell it.

Smell it and know she was his. And she belonged to him. But he knew this was only his ego speaking. He knew it was arrogant to think any woman would go to such lengths or that God would be so cruel as to make a man believe a woman would do such a thing.

Yet, this line of thinking always made him smile because she was exactly the kind of woman who would go to such lengths. And as for God – well, everyone knows what a sick sense of humor He was known to have. He remembered her frustration when she learned early on in their relationship that he would never allow her to share any of what he considered his personal burdens or problems. Whether they be financial or medical in nature, as far as he was concerned, they were his burdens to bear, and his alone.

In this regard, he was and would always be a relatively private man. She had turned away from him dejected and wounded at the reality of the shackles he had placed upon their relationship. She was the kind of woman who wanted to be needed and included in all aspects of her partner's life. She needed more than anything to be needed by him, and he wanted her more than anything he had wanted in a long while. Unfortunately, over the years his heart had become as scarred and calloused as his carpenter's work-worn hands.

She could be childish at times, which annoyed him because he had never once been capable of laughing easily or of finding many moments of levity in life.

She was not a stupid woman, but at times he just could not help feeling as if he had missed the joke. Yet, she could see through the façade he often displayed to the world. And of course, his erratic visits and lack of continuous displays of affection or affirmation of his feelings had annoyed and vexed her, just as it probably would any other woman. But still, underneath it all, and in spite of it all, she was there.

Oftentimes she was probably kicking herself in the head for seeming to be waiting on him to get his shit together, but not once did she ever give him cause to think she wanted or needed to be with someone else. Something inside of her just accepted the fact he was not the most affectionate or forthcoming of men. She was a woman who had found no shame in appreciating the time he would afford her. He could not say it and never would, but the time, those moments of quiet intimacy were harder for him to give than anyone other than himself would ever know.

She often went fishing for verbal affirmations of his affection and believed in his unspoken love, and for this, he was grateful. There simply was no lengthy poetry in Terris, and hell would be well frozen over before he penned a letter of affection to any female. So, he would be forever grateful to whatever unseen force reminded her of the feelings he carried for her. He would never know how or why; she just seemed to sense there was some other unknown voice scratching at his thoughts and dreams.

She never asked him about it, and never blamed him for his inability to find the words to explain it. At one point, it had actually pained him not to know whether he would ever be able to settle his thoughts and be with her. But, for some unknowable reason, it had not pained him quite as much as he thought it ought to – not if he really loved her. Terris could be likened to a gladiator who lived by the codes of men: strength, honor, and duty in all things. Live as a warrior; die as a man.

While both could appreciate the love found in a woman's eyes, neither could tolerate the worry that also laid there, the concern in her eyes or the heavy burden that loving a woman brings. And although he found most women to be quite tedious, he had fallen in love with this one despite himself.

And, this in spite of knowing there were certain things to being a self-respecting man a woman could never fully come to understand. He had stopped trying to explain this fact to the fairer sex some thirty odd years ago. A woman could never understand the "whys" of a man, just as she could never hear the voice inside his head directing him as clearly and unquestionably as any compass needle pointing true North.

It was a voice that said, "This is what a man does. This is how a man acts. This is how a man carries himself and carries his load in life. This is what a man is – and a man is what you are."

That voice, that mantra or creed, or whatever you call it, is a thing not made by a woman or for her to understand. This directive was a man's religion, and all any man ever needed was a woman who could maintain her faith in a thing she knew she would never come to understand. Faith of this kind didn't come easy to a woman like Valerie.

Something to the left of his sternum tightened at the mere thought of her name. He could hear the consonants in his head as clearly as if he had spoken them aloud. The "something" just to the left of his sternum became a knot at the base of his heart. He felt his jaw muscles tighten and the blood surge to his face. In that moment, he hated himself for allowing her name to be remembered, the name of a woman who had done nothing to deserve being forgotten.

He shook his head violently, as if doing so would shake loose and fling the thought of her from his mind and his heart. He had already come very close to taking a nasty (and most likely permanent) fall by just thinking her name! It had instantly knocked him from his center of being, and this was something he could not afford to do, not here on the side of some obscure mountain in China. Not if he wanted to survive. Survival. The thought would save him. Survival is the one thing a man can justify, discarding all other thoughts for its sake.

It had begun to snow. How long ago it started, he could not be sure. He looked around and was surprised to see he was about a hundred yards away from an outcropping of trees.

All was silent, aside from the occasional sound of a few birds. The sky had turned a cold, slate grey, and to his relief there was no wind to seep underneath his garments and stab him with its icy breath. He had no doubt that despite his reasonably good health, his knee and hip joints would eventually have plenty to say about this little adventure.

Dear God, what and I doing? Where am I? Who am I?

His mind began to wander and he thought perhaps the cold and desolation of the place was causing him to approach the limits of what remained of his sanity. His only thought, past the need to survive, was that he must take the time to remember. Remember all that had occurred to him up to this point, this moment and the moment that had just passed. It was The Voice, the Man Directive, if you will, telling him it was important he remember these things.

The wind picked up and the snow fell steadily as Terris trudged in it knee deep, turning slightly now and again toward the east to remain parallel with a sparse tree line running approximately eight-hundred yards off to his right. As he approached the tree line itself, he looked up through the ancient barrier of the pine trees toward the snow-covered peaks of the Tian Shan, or what the more reverent of the local population referred to as the "Celestial Mountains."

From where he was standing, Terris could clearly see a narrow ledge protruding from the side of the slope nearest to his location. How close to the ground it actually was, he could not tell from his current vantage point. Were he able to imagine wildlife in this place, he would have guessed the ledge could easily accommodate an agile bobcat or a snow leopard.

Terris briefly wondered if they even had snow leopards in China; he couldn't remember the last time he had actually watched National Geographic or anything like that.

He could see that the ledge seemed to lead toward a narrow crevasse and perhaps, he hoped, the crevasse was camouflaging the entrance to a cave.

He thought a cave might just suit him for the evening, just long enough to get warm, perhaps long enough for him to remember whatever it was he was supposed to remember; he couldn't be sure.

It took him the better part of an hour to make his way to the ledge once he found a decent spot to access it from the forest floor. He had to free climb thirty feet, or so, up the craggy base of the mountain to reach the ledge, but once there, his initial speculation proved to be correct. The ledge was packed thick with snow, but not as slippery as he initially thought it might be, and it was slightly wider than he had anticipated, enough for him to walk straight forward if he so chose and inch his way along the mountainside.

Terris was starting to believe the ledge almost wrapped around the mountain, but before this thought ran too far ahead of itself, the ledge ended abruptly at what appeared to be a crevasse, which then opened up into a sort of hollow. Terris managed to wedge his modest but sturdy frame into the narrow space of the crevasse. The rocky sides of the alcove cut the brunt of the winds racing up that side of the mountain. He sat with his back pressed firmly against the rock wall and found there was just enough room to extend his legs. It didn't matter because there was still enough of a gust to cause him to draw his knees up to his chest to conserve his body heat.

His thirty plus years of martial arts training and the exhaustive workouts that came along with it subsequently kicked in, allowing him to block out any lingering thoughts he was beginning to have about being cold and possibly freezing to death.

He found it easy to disregard the cold on his face and in his feet as it seeped through his insulated pants and up his tailbone. A part of him knew the danger of denying the truth. He could sit here in this spot for twelve hours or more, not feeling a thing. But he couldn't stop the effects of the bitter cold on his flesh. Not really, not in the real world.

In less than five hours there would be pain in his toes, fingers, face, and legs and his brain most likely would be unable to ignore it. The pain would then peak and go away before numbness set in and the cells of his flesh began to deteriorate and die. Then, he would be stuck here, literally a black frozen Popsicle on the side of some uncharted part of a mountain range in China. Not a good way for any self-respecting brother to go. But perhaps it was already too late.

His eyes were closed but he couldn't manage to pinpoint the moment when he had actually closed them. He could hear the wind howling viciously through the upper portion of the crevasse in which he sat, and if he craned his neck just so, he could see the snow blustering past the opening through which he had narrowly squeezed. He couldn't recall the final moments of his climb into a crack on the backside of what was quickly becoming a frozen hell.

A hell he knew, one he had chosen to come to, but for the life of him – and he had a strong feeling that in the end it would cost him exactly that – he couldn't think of or remember the how or the goddamned why of any of it. And now he was being forced to remember. Not the journey or the inclination that had led him to come here. No, it was the voice, the voice in his head, the "thing" that wanted him to remember a certain day.

It was a day in his life some forty odd years ago, Friday, September 26, 1981 to be exact. It was the day he decided he was no longer going to be on the receiving end of his father's strap because of the shenanigans of his fast-talking older brother, John Louis, who everybody called "Preacher." The elder Mr. Jackson, who was a former merchant marine, was well known for four things: his faith in God, his patience, his strong hands, and his accuracy in hitting someone's backside with whatever household item he could get his hands on, to use as a corrective device to punish any one of his nine children upon losing his aforementioned patience.

This decision freed Terris' precious behind from his father's curative wrath and ultimately set the tone for the man he would one day become. The voice in his head didn't want the specifics, but only remembrance of the feelings the day had brought along with it. The feelings revolved around the calmness of spirit he experienced as he watched John Louis intentionally break into old Mrs. Rainey's car window with a brick.

He saw the twenty-dollar bill lying on the driver's seat, and the moment John Louis spotted it. Terris briefly argued the point that since the bill was inside the old lady's car, it was technically her money.

John Louis, however, argued that since the lady didn't know it was there, why not take it? It was as dumb an argument as any the then nine-year-old Terris had ever heard.

Far too dumb for him to take an ass whipping for, especially since he didn't agree with the deed and was fairly certain his brother had no intention of coming off with one dime of the money. He clearly remembered watching John Louis throw the brick at the passenger window and how completely unlike the movies it had been. The glass had not shattered into a gazillion shimmering pieces like it did in the Charles Bronson films he loved so much. All it did was crack and fold inward as though the glass had been glued to some invisible board before being mounted onto the car. And somehow, to Terris, it seemed as if the crack snaked across the window in slow motion.

He heard John Louis say the "S" word. Funny, here he was a middle-aged black man freezing his balls off in a crack on the side of a mountain, thinking with the mind of a nine-year-old. Funny.

A moment of clarity drifted back to his mind and spirit like a balm, to the moment on that Friday afternoon on September 26, 1981 when he became aware of what was right and what was wrong. Of what it meant for one to decide, to make the choice to not be just a part of the world, but to take part in it. The moment he realized there existed something deeper and more vital than greed or pride, something grander than the self-righteous lie all Mankind had come to call the "Id."

Because in that odd moment, as the crack in the gleaming window of the automobile coursed across the pane with a sound like a whining child, John Louis, the older brother Terris would have happily followed through the gates of hell without question – fell from grace.

Terris flinched as he remembered the sound, coupled with the memory of the joyous look on Mrs. Rainey's face that Sunday morning right before church, when her two years hence dead husband had presented her with the car. He recalled how wonderfully clean the car had been on that day, how highly polished and pristine. And hadn't it always been so? His father told him it took a special kind of handy work to get a car to shine like that and keep it that way.

It was called a "military shine," the kind of shine that was worked into a man and not taught to him. It was the kind of shine a man could take pride in having done well, if it was done right. Now, Mr. Rainey had been dead for some time and his wife was well past sixty. For the first time ever, Terris pondered who had been keeping the car so beautifully clean all those years. At that moment, he put the final pieces of the puzzle together and lost all feeling in his butt and on down.

The only other car on the block so highly polished was his father's own beloved 1973 burnt coral Buick Riviera – the car he bought the very year Terris was born. Hadn't he heard Mr. Rainey and his father talking about the price of cars one Saturday morning with his own ears about a month before Mrs. Rainey's four-wheeled gem showed up? Dear Christ, he and John Louis might as well be vandalizing their father's car!

And if they were going to do that, well then, they might as well go ahead and start running toward Mexico!

John Louis had picked up another brick but Terris was on him like butter on a bowl of grits before he could throw it, and the older boy was caught completely off-guard by the blitz attack. John Louis fell over sideways, bewildered, befuddled and mad as hell as his younger brother wrestled the brick from his hands, screaming over and over, "No! No! Johnny, Stop it! Just stop! It's not right!"

Terris lost the fight. John Louis was a whole foot and a half taller, a whole lot faster, and would have rather died than be beaten in public, let alone in broad daylight by his younger brother. John Louis got the brick and the better of Terris by bloodying his younger brother's nose and busting his lip. To make matters even worse, Mrs. Rainey witnessed the entire thing.

When she stepped onto her porch armed with a broom, both boys scrambled to their feet. John Louis dropped the brick at his brother's feet and ran.

Terris stood facing the elderly woman with her upraised broom and tears running down her ample cheeks. He felt a deep and unfamiliar sense of shame that made him want to die right there on the spot. But he stood his ground and looked at the old widow right in the eye.

That moment changed his life, although perhaps not in the way one would expect. He did not become a "godly" man at this point, and he would never be, nor would he ever qualify as a Boy Scout.

He would never harbor any latent thoughts or regrets about joining a church. Yet, this particular event was one of the defining moments of his life, because he became unafraid to face the consequences of any actions he chose to take from that point forward. This was the moment when his young mind and old spirit realized there was no mortal man of whom he would ever have need to fear.

Mrs. Rainey stood silently, purposefully, looking at him. She held her broom firmly in one hand, in the event the young hoodlum decided to do something stupid. But she knew he wouldn't. She knew this young man, the second of the nine or so crumb-snatchers belonging to the Jackson household. She shook her head and wondered at the ignorance of any woman who would have so many offspring well before her fiftieth birthday. But this thought was gone almost as soon as she thought it.

She and her late husband had been intimate a grand total of three times during their forty-plus years of a childless marriage. Both had found out quite early on in their marriage that they were not as fond of a traditional union, as either of them had initially thought. But on one thing they did agree, three times in the hay were two too many times for either of them. She and Arthur had not wanted children, and it wasn't long after they had exchanged vows that she discovered her new husband wasn't particularly fond of women. It was of little consequence because she, Gloria, happened to be very fond of women. They had met and married in their small church, and that church is where they kept their solace (and their secrets) throughout their amicable union.

Arthur told his secrets to the elder deacon, and Gloria kept her secrets with the same deacon's wife. In the end, it made for two extremely content marriages and four happy parishioners. But times were as different now as they had been back then. At the moment, she was sorting out what to do with the sturdy little heathen standing before her. She had seen what his older brother had done, because she lit a cigarette and watched from the shadows of her living room as the older boy briefly laid out his plan – moments before chucking a brick at the passenger window of her car. She wasn't particularly upset about the window.

Unbeknownst to any of the neighbors, his act gave her a reason to leave the house. She rarely had an occasion to do so, as there was little to no unexpected events in the life of a widowed lesbian who had managed to outlive both her husband and her lover, and therefore, her church.

The 1973 four-door, emerald-green Cadillac held a double-edged sentiment for her. She had coveted the car for damn near a year, as it sat on the dealership lot on Stony Island Avenue. She longed for it every Sunday after church that summer when she and Arthur would go up to the Moo and Oink to get meat for their evening supper. She wanted the car badly. She could not, however, say the same for the cold sores beginning to appear in uncomfortable places after Arthur had returned from one of the church's all-male retreats. Those she had not wanted … and she let him know it in no uncertain terms. But she did want that car.

Arthur had only driven it once – on the day he gave it to her. The car was a token of an apology for the physical discomfort he had unwittingly caused her, a discomfort she would never be free of for as long as she lived. A discomfort she acquired shortly after indulging in the third and the last of his heterosexual delusions, which she hadn't minded because she loved him.

The truth was, Arthur had been her best friend, her very best friend, and for more than forty years, they lived and loved each other as such. Each contentedly married, they were both quite happily and very secretly gay.

But this was in the past, and this boy, the one they called "Little Terry," he was the present. Here and now and the business of the broken window was foremost in her mind at the moment. She expected the boy to try and make a break for it, or at the very least, start stammering hopelessly through the myriad lame-ass lies and excuses all kids seem to have. But the boy remained silent and his gaze remained steadfast. Gloria would think back on the encounter often prior to her death some years later, still silently impressed by the boy's willingness to accept the situation for what it was.

"Well?" she said, noticing Terris' eyes were looking at the broom she was holding.

"I'm sorry about your window, Mrs. Rainey. I tried to stop him, but ..."

"But you got your ass whooped. Yeah, I saw the whole thing. That brother of yours, the one they call "Preacher" – he's gonna get your little black butt in a world of trouble. I ought to call the police."

Terris just stared at her; he knew she was lying. Black folks rarely ever called the police on their own, especially not on a little kid.

It wasn't as if he had murdered her dog or anything. Gloria was well aware he knew her threat was an empty one. She had no reason to wish an early death upon the child, and they both knew if the police didn't manage to beat him within an inch of his life, his father most certainly would. Still, she had mentioned the police, so technically it was still her move.

"You come on in the house with me until I decide what I'm going to do with you," said Gloria. "Either way though, you best get ready to pay me what I got coming to get that window fixed."

"Yes, Ma'am," Terris replied with more than a little relief. The woman had not mentioned his father, so as far as he was concerned, things were going rather well.

The old woman almost smiled as she watched him throw his narrow, little shoulders back and hold his head up high as he marched up the front stairs past her and into the house.

He looked as though he were a man who had made peace with his impending demise before standing in front of a firing squad. The house was dark but clean and what most would consider a bit too warm.

But Terris' mother had often talked about how old folks get to "runnin" cold," as she put it, something to do with their blood getting thin. As far as he was concerned, the house was like stepping into a warm mitten, and he didn't mind it one bit because he had always been partial to heat.

Everything in the modest living room was perfect – the piano, the vase of flowers, the antiquated furniture, even the dark, burgundy rug. The sunlight shining through the sheer curtains illuminated the dust in the air. Gloria made her way past him and leaned the broom against the wall before shuffling down the hall toward the kitchen.

"You thirsty?"

"No, Ma'am"

"Well, I got me this lemonade made. My husband used to drink it all the time. I can't stand the stuff, too sweet for me. Don't know why I keep making it, really; I mean it's not like he's coming back, right?"

"No, Ma'am"

"No, I suppose he ain't. Here, drink up," she said as she pushed a full glass of lemonade toward his face.

The boy snatched the glass from her and eagerly drank the yellow liquid. She made a "hrmmph" sound as if to say she knew all along that he had first refused the drink out of politeness.

"Sit down. Now, you know I'm gonna have to talk with your Daddy, don't you?"

"I figured you would. But that's alright, I should've been faster, and I could've stopped him. Anyway, it won't be the first beating I get because of John Louis."

"Well, that might be so, but as far as I can see, that brother of yours is big enough to take his own beatings."

"Yeah, but I'll get it because I'm the one who got caught. John Louis don't never own up to nothing he ain't caught doing red-handed. And well, Ma'am, I ain't no snitch!"

"Oh, I can tell! You too smart to be a snitch. You should've just cut and run like your brother did. Why didn't you?"

"I dunno – just didn't seem right. I mean, you ain't never done nothing to us, and John Louis can just be plain mean sometimes."

"Well, I'll deal with Mr. John Louis later, in my own way and in my own time. Don't you worry about that! In the mean-time, you wash out that glass and then get yourself on out of here. I got something to do."

"But what about your window?"

"I'll put the car in the garage soon, but you come and see me first thing in the morning. Maybe you can ride along with me to get it fixed, seeing as how you owe me for what it's gonna cost me to fix it."

Terris did go back the next day and every day after that for the remainder of the summer and the next. Mrs. Rainey had indeed called Mr. Jackson and detailed the actions of his eldest son. She also related the sound judgment recently acquired by the son the elder Jackson called "Lil' Terry." As a result of the conversation, Terris got the privilege of shaking his father's hand for the first time "as a man."

It was the handshake of mutual respect that would be retained and shared between a father and his grown son in future years.

As far as Terris was concerned, the handshake was the most valuable thing he had ever earned, and he was determined to keep it for the rest of his life.

John Louis, on the other hand, received the long overdue butt tanning of his young life and had to sit on a pillow for a week. Mr. Jackson made it clear to everyone who could hear him over the older boy's hollering and wailing that John "Preacher" Louis was receiving a hefty "payment forward" on any future devilment he might be considering.

Terris spent the next four summers doing odd jobs for Mrs. Rainey under the military-style tutelage of his father. This included mowing the lawn with a rolling blade push mower, despite Mrs. Rainey having offered the use of her electric one.

After patching and painting the old lady's garage, his father began to work the coveted skill into young Terris of washing and then coaxing a shine onto 1973 emerald-green Cadillac. A shine soon became the second highest military shine of any car on the block because no one would ever outshine Buick Riviera.

On the Saturday evening when Terris achieved bringing out the shine on Mrs. Rainey's car all by himself, he showed up at the dinner table carrying the brick John Louis had used to break the car window.

The whole family was about to be seated and remained silent as Terris placed the brick on John Louis chair. No one, not even his father said a word as John Louis came to sit down but was forced to pick up the brick from his chair before taking his place at the table. No one looked at him as he stared wide-eyed at Terris.

John Louis sat down, and their father and mother started laughing, which made John Louis laugh too. Then Terris and the rest of his seven brothers and sisters joined their family in laughing out loud.

John Louis even complemented Terris on what a fine job he had done on the Cadillac and admitted he had already warned the entire neighborhood to keep their distance because it was his little brother's ride now. This was the last time he and John Louis ever tussled; his big brother eventually grew up and became a top advertising executive at Ebony magazine before opening a private art gallery in Somerset, New York.

Once, when Terris was bullied at school and beaten up by three older boys, it was Mrs. Rainey's house he went to first. His father still had some pretty specific ideas about how to handle any of his sons if and when they ever lost a fight. Terris hadn't been particularly keen on having two beatings on the same day, especially since he had only just recently earned a modicum of respect from his father.

Mrs. Rainey hadn't coddled or babied him; she merely asked if he had started it and took him at his word when he told her that he had not.

Then, she did something odd – she instructed him to taste the blood was still drying at the corner of his mouth. He gave her a look as though he thought she must be joking, but the glare she gave him in return let him know she was deadly serious.

"Ain't too tasty, is it?" she asked solemnly.

"No," he sulked, thinking she was mocking his defeat, and he suddenly regretted having taken refuge in her home.

"Good. No man should like the taste of his own blood and that's the last time I want you to have occasion to, ya hear? Come on, let's get you cleaned up."

Without another word, she cleaned him up and gave him three crisp one-dollar bills out of her purse.

"What's this for?" he asked.

"I want you to take me some place and as the man, you got to pay for it, not me."

Before he could ask where they were going, she had put on her coat and Sunday hat and shuffled him out of the door and into her prized Cadillac. She drove fast and with silent determination. Even though he had been in the car with her many times before, he knew this excursion was somehow different, and that silence was probably the safest recourse. She drove them to the Rialto Theater clear on the other side of town and marched him up to the ticket window, where he purchased two matinee tickets to see a foreign movie called *Return of The Dragon*.

The movie featured a slender Chinese man who was not particularly muscular doing things that seemed like magic to a twelve-year-old, inner city boy.

Mrs. Rainey had introduced him to the world of martial arts. Seeing a man of such small stature standing up to those who were not only trying to oppress him, but who also outnumbered him resonated with Terris. Three months later, on his thirteenth birthday, he began to train.

Thirty-five years and numerous street fights later, he was a thirteen-time world champion with a seventh-degree black belt. His martial arts training provided a discipline that instilled in him a sense of pride and accomplishment. He had lived in three different states during his adult life and had been required to register his hands as "lethal weapons" in each of them.

He and every other person of color in America knew it was only meant to provide yet another loophole by which some over-zealous cop could shoot his way through an unarmed brown or black man, should he find himself unlucky enough to be on the wrong side of an officer's gun.

On the few occasions in his life when he'd had the unfortunate luck of having to deal with law enforcement, he would often amuse himself with a mental game he liked to call, "How Many Ways Can This Situation Go Left?"

His friendship with Mrs. Rainey taught him the value of having a trade and the hard work that came with it. An uncle on his father's side was a carpenter, and by the time Terris was fifteen, his weekends were spent working with his hands. He was awed by the simplicity of his hands having the power to destroy or restrain through martial arts, and also to create, repair or heal, depending on the nature of the man who wields the tools or the hands.

The Creator had shifted the destiny of a young boy through the shards of a cracked passenger window of an old lady's car. His ways were indeed mysterious and unfathomable.

And now, in this moment on this mountain over forty years later, it was plain to Terris that even the old lady had been in on his conversion.

But he had walked away from that life. Walked away from the land of his birth and the woman he loved to travel alone into this remote mountain range. It was a journey he had to make, to somehow make his way to a snowcapped mountain on the other side of the world – to find what? He simply did not know. But he had to try. If he didn't, he knew the sound of the deeply intoned bell continually chiming inside his head night and day for nearly six years would eventually drive him to fire a bullet into his skull just to stop its baleful call.

In an instant, he was with Valerie again and the memory of her filled his head. He felt, wrongly so, that were he to move his mouth, he would instantly feel the pressure of her lips against his own. He would breathe in the warm breath she exhaled through her nostrils. He would feel the tip of her warm tongue seeking his own and would respond in kind. And then she would laugh. He had never known why; perhaps it was something she retained from her own fading youth.

Her laugh both annoyed and delighted him; annoying him because whenever she laughed when their lips parted, he looked at her and could never keep from smiling himself. He smiled at the modest gap between her two front teeth and smiled at whatever lingering girlish silliness had made her laugh in the first place.

In the moment of their kiss, her laugh and his smile, she knew he would not chastise her for being who and what she was – a teenager trapped inside the body of a middle-aged woman. A woman who awakened one day unable to fathom where all the years had gone. Terris shook his head to clear the smell of her from his mind. He would not bring her here to this place on the backside of beyond. Not here, not now.

He was hearing something, though. Something ... a sound ... a hum? A song? Something just underneath the blustering wind. A hum. His eyes remained closed and he stilled his body to tune into the direction of the sound.

It was coming from somewhere off to his right, somewhere not far beyond the crevasse in which he sat. But it wasn't a hum; it was a chant.

A chant, faint, indistinct and ethereal. A steady chanting made by the voices of men. Yes, he could hear a steady phonetic mantra winding its way through the rising wind. He knew this sound; he knew it well, because he had often teased a woman who was over five thousand miles away about the very thing he was now hearing. A woman he had just been thinking of and who could not possibly know anything of this place. A chant she uttered daily in the name of a religion he did not, and had not wanted to understand. A chant now right here with him in this place, on this mountain, in a fucking crack in a rock, being uttered by faceless voices on the wind.

Terris opened his eyes and was only mildly surprised by the thin layer of ice that had formed on his cheeks and across the bridge of his nose. He had no way of knowing how much time had passed. How long it had been since night had fallen on the Tian Shan, but now the snow-laden surface of the mountain glistened beneath a ceiling of unfiltered starlight.

The night sky was like a cache of diamonds cradled in rich, black velvet, and it was easy to understand how a man could crane his neck toward the heavens for hours trying to take it all in in a pathetic attempt to understand how it all came to be.

His visual reverie was enhanced by the continuous underlying hum of the disembodied chanting, which was steady, fluid and entreating.

Terris knew he had been compelled to come to this cold, isolated and deceptively desolate place perhaps for the sole purpose of hearing the chant at this time. The warm glow of self-realization moved through his loins. He knew he had been called by something larger than himself, and he had heard and responded to it. Something inside of him instinctively knew this, in and of itself, yes, even this, him sitting in this crack was indeed a great achievement.

He shifted his weight as he steadied himself upon legs that had grown stiff with age and reluctant with the cold. He grimaced hard beneath the two woolen scarves covering his face. He was sorely reminded of his mortality and age as the muscles in his lower back protested painfully at having to move. But his spirit would not be denied. The internal compass set in motion by an unseen hand now had its needle pointed toward the source of the chanting.

He steadied himself once again upon the narrow ledge by bracing his back on the hard rock face of the crevasse.

The sound seemed to generate from an area to his right somewhere on the far side of the crevasse. Terris carefully inched his way further along the uneven ledge jutting out from the wall of rock.

The surface here was full of fresh snow and as slick as ice slate. He noticed the sudden drop in temperature and to his dismay he realized that if he were forced to spend the night on the ledge, he would most likely be dead before morning.

He could already feel the cold piercing his outerwear like so many frozen daggers. But the chanting continued to rise above the wind and his growing disdain; as long as it did, the least he could do was try to meet it halfway.

As if confirming his thoughts, he heard the distinctive sound of a temple singing bowl, yet another thing he was familiar with – thanks to the woman he loved. The long, low voice of the bowl reverberated gently through the narrow space in which he now found himself. Terris felt his first real moment of alarm when he looked up and saw two-hundred-foot rock walls rising on either side of him.

The moon was full, and its rays provided a false light as it reflected off the microscopic surface of the fresh, fallen snow. Through watery eyes, Terris could just barely make out large, ominous clumps of snow precariously clinging here and there over the many unseen rock outcroppings protruding high above his head. They seemed to dare him to give a reason for them to come crashing down and bury him forever.

Any reason, at all, a misstep, a grunt or even the seemingly gentle vibrations caused by the ringing of a not-so-far-off Buddhist temple singing bowl.

The narrow passage he followed toward the sound of the chanting became even narrower, and his head began to fill with the sound, which seemed somehow compressed at the narrowest point between the two walls of solid rock. His head soon felt like the clapper of a bell.

The maddening aspect was that the voices of those who chanted were no louder than they had been some hours before. Closer, yes, but no louder. He shuddered at the uncertainty of not understanding the whys and how comes of his current situation.

He did not know what to think or how to process it, but something within him knew it was wrong. He let the thought go before it could make him sweat. Sweating out here could lead to pneumonia, which would lead to his death out here in the middle of the backside of beyond. No thought was worth that much trouble.

Upon reaching the narrowest point of the passage, he surmised it was too close of a space for him to feasibly get through. He felt the cold hand of fear clutching and squeezing at his heart. For the briefest of moments, he fully expected to feel the forsaken agony of a cardiac arrest.

Instead, his heart and mind were filled with an inconsolable sense of sorrow and longing. Everything inside him, all that he was, desperately needed to pass this point.

He needed to reach the source of the sound now filling his head. He needed to reach it or die trying.

And then it stopped. The chanting stopped abruptly as if someone had snatched a plug from the wall. To his horror, he felt as if his heart would stop just as suddenly. The silence fell upon him like a shroud.

Even the high-pitched whine of the mountain winds failed to penetrate the bubble of silence in which he stood. Without thinking, he began to peel away the layers of clothing and abstract scarves and pieces of cloth cocooning his body. Every rational thought that remained screamed for him to stop. But he did not. He could not.

Naked and cold, but extremely strong-willed, if not exactly altogether physically sturdy, a middle-aged black man birthed himself from that narrow passage and out onto an upper cleft of stone jutting outward high above a snow-laden valley. Terris had emptied out the contents of his pack and thrown them through the narrow opening ahead of him. But even after only a brief time exposed to the elements, his hands and fingers had grown so cold and numb that he was unable to gather up his belongings or immediately put his clothes back on. He felt as if wanted to lay down and rest, but he knew the urge was merely his brain starting to die – the simplistic strategy of a body that could take no more.

His burly, callous-ridden hands had already unconsciously formed into tightly clutched fists. It was an exercise in agony as he bent his body over to retrieve his pants from the ground, and when he did bend over, a bomb suddenly exploded between his legs.

It felt as though a large and extremely angry mule with a grudge had kicked him from behind with its hoof landing directly on his exposed testicles.

He screamed like an eight-year-old girl, a high-pitched scream none would believe a man such as he capable of making. All at once, everything went blurry and bile rose thickly in his throat. His felt his precious gonads make a gallant run for the border by retracting from the cold and causing an indescribable sciatic cramp. He lay in a fetal position on the cold ground, buck-naked except for the pants bunched around his ankles. He knew he had to get up, despite the fact his testicles had probably retreated so far into his asshole that he could no longer be considered a man.

"No!" he screamed in defiance. His lungs felt like they were filled with battery acid instead of oxygen. The center of his head felt like it had been penetrated by a cold, steel blade.

His body shuddered violently, and he knew there was a good chance of it being the last command his brain would issue before he dropped dead. He was in the throws of death, and he knew it.

"Not like this ...," he mumbled through frozen lips. He was naked and afraid and pissed off all at the same time. But it was this last emotion – anger – that gave him the will to get up. He simply would not allow himself to die in the ass crack of a mountain. He could not bear the thought of not being found. Or worse, being found and having the bizarre circumstance of his demise attributed to an alien abduction or some such nonsense.

This thought angered him; he had always promised himself that he would die an "honorable" death – whatever that meant in this day and age. At any rate, freezing to death was not one of the options. With every ounce of will remaining in him, he managed to get on his haunches. A feeble, squatting position was all his extremities could achieve in the bitter cold. His trousers remained tightly clutched in one clenched and nearly frozen, albeit gloved fist.

Every move was a symphonic agony as he pulled on his trousers and got back into his coat. His suffering was such that he had begun to sob.

His lungs felt as though he were breathing fire, and the pain and effort it took for him to pull his boots back on brought him close to blacking out.

He could not recall exactly when he'd lost all the feeling in his toes, but he was quite aware none of them had snapped off while he redressed them. He managed to pull his boots on, still not sure whether all of his toes had survived the ordeal. Afterwards, he crawled on all fours to reach his supply pack a few feet away, and that's when it happened.

The faintest wisp of warm air brushed across his forehead. It wasn't much ... but ... it ... was. He crawled to the spot where his pack had lain and again felt the slight change in temperature.

He went further still, despite the wind and snow biting at his exposed flesh. His swollen eyes were functional enough for him to see the solid black rock that had replaced the unforgiving ice and snow on which he had been traveling.

He could not stand, and somewhere within him, he was certain he might never do so again. But here was a vent of warmth, so he inched further toward the unseen oasis like a blind and hapless baby seeking its mother's breast. The skin on his face and ears seared with pain, and in this way, he knew the warmth was no mere trick of a dying brain. At least, he hoped not.

Just then, Terris had the very first conscious, ethereal experience of his life. Someone or something outside of his Id spoke to him. "Look and see," the voice said. He heard the words somewhere deep within the chambers of his burning chest as if they had emanated from the very center of his being. Yet, he knew neither the words nor the voice were his own. His stomach clenched in absolute terror and he became motionless.

"Look and see," the words reverberated through Terris' body a second time. He knew he was on the verge of collapse and quite probably death. And in the same instant, he uncharacteristically conceded that if these were to be his last moments on Earth, then so be it.

With what little life was left within him, he lifted his bleary eyes toward the sky and did his level best to peer through the grey veil of flurrying snow swirling around him like a swarm of a million tiny tornados.

He could see nothing and was unable to make out so much as the narrow lip of the crevasse upon which he now crawled. This was it. This was where he was going to die. Lost ... and alone.

And it was this reality of the solitude of his impending demise that caused a painful knot to form somewhere deep in his guts. A knot, or spasm – or some form of intestinal death rattle. Whatever – all he knew was he felt as though what little "spark" of life was left in him was being snuffed out.

His face burned, and when he had fallen on his back, the left side of his chest felt as if someone had fired a large cannonball through it. When he coughed, he realized an unseen hand had also fully gutted him with a bowing knife – because of the thick, nearly frozen blood spewing from his mouth like a bitter pudding. He raised the back of his hand to wipe off his mouth before thinking about what he was doing. His bottom lip separated and split when he did so, and another fresh spurt of blood flowed from his ripped mouth as he whimpered like a regretful child. What little sight he had remaining only registered the cold grey world around him.

He was no longer aware of his feet, and he was willing to bet at least two of his toes were rattling around somewhere inside the confines of his boot, completely independent of his foot. He was also fairly confident his fingers were going to follow suit as he made the decision to get to his feet. Because he would die on his feet if he could.

If by some great mercy, God would allow him to. If God could even understand how important it was to a man of no particular importance, the manner in which he died. Even here, even now. Even if no one ever knew how or when or why, and even if "she" would never know, the thought of it hurt him more than he believed it ever could.

There was one thing he did know: his woman – if indeed that was what Valerie still was – knew him, and she would expect nothing less of him. If he could give her nothing else, or himself for that matter, in this moment, he would somehow manage to die on his feet and God's will be damned! Melodramatic as it might be, he would at least do that! Mostly because the one thing he wanted, and someday intended to do, he now realized he could not. He could not answer the question of "why" he had been compelled to come all this way only to die. Fifty-four-year-old Terris Jackson used the very last of his strength to crawl to his feet on the side of a snow-covered desolate mountain in China.

He spread his aching and most likely frostbitten arms out to his sides as though intending to take flight.

"I love you," were the last words he attempted to utter from the two cracked and frozen pieces of flesh that were once his lips. But the soft tissue of his face, mouth and throat were now grossly swollen and had been frozen shut hours ago.

His mouth spewed forth blood in place of well-meaning words. No sound or breath came forth. He simply fell forward off the lip of the narrow ledge into the thick mist below the ledge where he had been crouched only a moment before. Once his feet left the edge of the ledge, Terris craned his head slightly to the right and thought he saw an expansive Japanese-style temple cradled in the palm of a lush, green valley, not five hundred yards from where he was now falling to his death.

Now he was finally sure he was dead, because he knew for a fact he was in China and not Japan, so there was that.

In the final milliseconds before Terris' body landed and he lost consciousness for good, he thought he saw a man dressed in dark robes emerge from the temple doors holding a lantern in one hand. He also thought the man looked directly at him, and that he might be Saint Peter ... and then Terris Jackson thought no more.

The Tyrin Speak

"And Whispered Softly"

As I watch the trees submerge beneath the morning mist.

So must my emotions descend beneath the blanket of my mind.

As the winds of change blow with the force that none can truly measure,

I turn my head to find a more soothing lecture.

And when the earth has fallen with time,

Death will have looked me in the eye.

But I will have heard,

The voice within,

Knowing that I was

Greater than

Most

...men.

5

Temple Khan Tengri

He came to consciousness enveloped in a black void, accompanied by nothing less than a mind-numbing level of agonizing pain in his flesh and bones, the likes of which Terris had never experienced in over a half-century of living. Could this be the Hell men lived in fear of for the better part of their lives? He could not help but wonder to what or whom he had performed such an atrocity to deserve such a fate. He didn't feel as though he was being burnt by fire, which was what he had anticipated or perhaps, even on some subconscious level, felt he deserved. But rather, his entire body, the core of his being, and his very soul had become like the exposed nerve of an angry and inflamed tooth in need of a root canal. He was neither hot nor cold; he was simply in excruciating pain and paralyzed with the overwhelming sensation of it.

Just as Terris thought his mind would soon slip into the depths of madness, he felt what he thought was someone gently touching a forefinger to the center of his forehead. As if a switch had been turned off, the pain in his body and mind stopped abruptly, and only the deep, peaceful darkness remained. He lay motionless – where he did not know, but at least there was no more pain.

He became aware he could now draw a breath, and he promptly did so, letting out a deep sigh, which unfortunately allowed some internal sharp-toothed beast to tear at his left lung.

This fresh assault on his nervous system was too much; Terris passed out before the unseen finger could once again flip the switch to make the pain go away.

When next he was aware of being conscious, he was still in complete darkness and he very slowly crept into his sense of self, as if having an out-of-body experience. He had the strangest feeling he was trying to "sneak up" on his own body. He was physically conscious of only a small space at the nape of his neck and of feeling a firm pressure across his eyes and forehead. He kept his sense of self contained in an effort not to provoke whatever toothy bastard had bitten him in the lung, Surely, it was still lurking somewhere nearby. But he still felt nothing else, no pain, no tightness, no limbs, no fingers, and no toes. He allowed his mind to explore his midsection and felt as though he was being embraced around his torso. The sensation of being held securely with no pain soon lulled him back to sleep, back into the recesses of his mind and the dark silence in which he now lived. His felt his body shifting without any effort on his part.

Although he felt no pain, the shift in position and the movement he sensed in the darkness about him had aroused him, and this time there was the distinct sound of a man's voice very near his face.

"Prop him up there," the gentle soft-spoken voice instructed as Terris felt himself being pivoted slightly onto his right side.

He could feel the firm pressure of at least two sets of hands on his back and hips. He tried to move what he thought was his head in protest, but his left arm flailed out and met with the neck of someone to his right.

"Ah, that's a good sign! Come now, here … try and take some broth." The voice was kind and patient, but all was still blackness for Terris, and he soon found he was unable to speak.

"It is too soon for words. Here … it's a straw; you must try and drink."

Terris felt the edge of a straw being gently but firmly pressed against his bottom lip. His mouth felt like it was stuffed with dry leaves. Still remembering the toothy beast that had tried to rip out his lung, he gingerly drew air through what he soon found was a somewhat unyielding wooden straw. The liquid that greeted his mouth was thick, hearty and warmed to the perfect temperature. It was neither too warm, nor too cool for his consumption.

It seemed flavorful and what little of it he gleaned greatly soothed the raw passage leading to his withered stomach. The elixir attempting to pass over his tongue and down his atrophied throat answered any lingering questions he had regarding his inability to speak. His tongue and throat were badly swollen, and the latter was nearly sealed shut. He was drowning! Goddamn it! He was drowning and no one was doing a damn thing about it!

Okay, Terris, calm down, keep your head, he thought to himself as he tried to assess the situation while he still had time.

Precious little time probably, but time, nonetheless. He didn't feel as though he was in water because he didn't feel wet. He gasped for air but now his mouth and throat were filled with liquid.

He could feel the distinct burn one felt as a child when swimming and water got into your lungs and those secret caverns of your sinuses. Inside. The "water" was coming from inside him.

When he tried to open his eyes, he realized he was drowning in his own fluid! The liquid death was coming from his lungs and spewing upwards like an uncapped geyser. He attempted to cough, which only resulted in a sensation he was certain wasn't unlike the feeling of having one's head blown off by a double-barreled, twelve-gauge shotgun!

And then, without warning, he heard the rustling of heavy fabric and the muffled sounds of a man calmly issuing what sounded like measured instructions. Once again, he felt himself being turned onto his right side effortlessly by whoever was bearing his weight. His body began the inevitable contortions of someone drowning.

Terris flailed against the three sets of hands he was sure were trying to restrain him. They held his arms at his side, and he felt a hand on either side of his head forcing it to turn to the right. He never felt the warmth of the Eucalyptus- infused steam suddenly present inches below his face.

But what he felt next did register, and it was a sensation he would not soon forget: release.

Without warning or effort, every passageway and sinus cavity opened up as if the swollen and congested flesh had been commanded to retreat. And with this retreat, he felt all the fluid trapped in his lungs, throat, mouth and nose rush forth as though he were a human geyser.

He could taste and smell the foul-smelling infected body fluid intermingled with the scent of what he assumed was some unpronounceable medicinal herb. It smelled of life – green and fresh. The thick-bile laden liquid expelled uncontrollably via his mouth and nose and through his nether regions of which he currently lacked both the energy and the pride with which to feel shame.

When the innate instinct to inhale overtook him, he did, and his lungs were at once filled with cool, life-sustaining fresh air. There proved to be many unseen but gentle hands to clean up after him. Terris was too exhausted and embarrassed to do anything more than allow the many unseen, charitable hands to clean and redress him in what seemed to be a mutually understood respectful silence, for which he was grateful. And it wasn't until Terris felt his ears decompress with an audible popping sound for a second time that the kind and melodious voice of a man at his right side spoke for the fourth time.

"There, that's it. Here, let me wipe your mouth. Okay, lay him back down. Gently...not so fast," said the sure and even-toned male voice.

Hands he could not see carefully laid him on his back. "My eyes … I can't see," explained Terris, jolting himself by the sound of his own voice. He could not begin to guess at how long it had been since he'd last spoken to another human being. *How long had he been on the mountain?*

He moved his hand toward his face; a hand that was heavy and thick, until he realized it was heavily bandaged.

A quick mental body check let him know both his feet were bandaged, as well. Upon reaching his face, he detected rather than felt soft gauze-like bandaging bound tightly over his eyes. Perhaps he was not completely blind, after all.

Just as he was about to attempt removal of the dressing, a small, soft hand touched his own and firmly moved it away from the bandage.

"Not yet my friend. Let us first draw the shutters. The damage from snow blindness can be unpredictable." It was the same reassuring male voice so Terris heeded the caution.

He sensed movement in the room and registered the presence of three people, as his soft-spoken caretaker left his side and someone exited the room. Terris was unable to track the movement of the third person but nonetheless was quite sure they remained nearby.

"Where am I?" Terris' voice sounded unfamiliar to him. His resonating baritone vocals sounded like gravel being crushed in his larynx. The pain was also not unlike the same image, so much so that it caused his breath to hitch, which gave way to a most unwelcome coughing fit. He could feel his eyes watering from the strain. Out of pain and frustration from his weakened state, he once again tried to remove the bandage from his eyes. He was again thwarted by swifter and stronger hands.

There was a brief power play between the unseen hands and his own. The former easily, albeit gently, exuded an inner strength much more powerful than his own.

Terris had not run across many he could recall who could dispel his physical will with so little effort. The hands released him and again the voice spoke.

"Here, this will ease the pain in your chest."

Terris felt the warmth of steam near his face. A small, cool clay cup with a sweet-smelling liquid was put into his bandaged hands and pushed toward his mouth.

"Drink. It will help. Paolo, draw the shutters please."

Terris drank as instructed and was silently grateful for whatever mystery brew filled the cup. He heard the distinct sound of wooden slats being adjusted and assumed it was the shutters fending off the dreaded sunlight.

The owner of the kind voice had not moved from his bedside, but he could hear the one called Paolo as he walked to each of the three slatted windows and adjusted the shutters.

The temperature in the room dropped slightly, but not uncomfortably, and everything became still except for a slight movement Terris could hear off to his right. Again, cautiously this time, he ventured, "Where am I?"

As if reciting a familiar bedtime tale to a child, the soft-spoken voice replied, as Terris felt nimble fingers begin to carefully remove the bandages on his eyes.

"You are in the Temple Khan Tengri in the Tian Shan Mountains."

"Khan Tengri?" Terris could not recall seeing this name on any map he had used.

Just then, the darkness lifted somewhat and he perceived faint fractals of light behind his closed eyelids.

The bandage was being unwrapped slowly and with care, as if his skull might halve at any moment causing his brains to plop out into his lap.

"You have been quite ill for several weeks. Your lungs were filled with fluid, and your hands and feet were severely frostbitten. You are fortunate to be alive."

The final layers of bandages were removed from Terris' head, and for a moment, the sensation made him feel completely exposed again. He kept his eyes closed despite his overwhelming curiosity about exactly where he was and exactly whom he was conversing with. He could feel the blood vessels in his face and neck refilling, now that the bandage restrictions were gone. The sensation made the tip of his nose tingle and twitch, and he instinctively reached up to scratch at his nose before he thought about what he was doing. The tip of his nose felt like a smooth leather knob protruding from the center of his face; it was numb, hard, and tight from snow burn.

While his caretakers remained silent and waited patiently, Terris continued to gingerly explore the surface of his face. The tops of his cheeks and the skin across the bridge of his nose were taut and tender beneath his fingertips. He made a feeble attempt to open his eyes, but he could not.

"Paolo," the voice that seemed to be in charge spoke, and Terris heard water sloshing around.

"Here," the owner of the voice placed a piece of soft water-soaked fabric into Terris' hands. It was warm and smelled strongly of rich, fertile earth.

Terris gently dabbed at the crusty remnants of mucus that had fused his eyes shut. For the briefest of moments, he marveled at the mechanics of the human body. A body that sought to protect a precious eyeball by fusing it shut against further assault or affliction. When he was at last capable of opening his eyes, he found himself face to face with something that looked to him as if it had stepped right out of Van Gogh's *The Scream*.

He blinked furiously to resuscitate his atrophied vision and dabbed at his eyes with the cloth again. He turned his head to the left, and again opened his eyes and found himself in a small, dimly lit room. The space was a rectangular shape, and just beyond the narrow bed upon which he had been placed, he could see a wooden table underneath a slatted window. Upon the table were the remnants of two well-used wax stick candles, which were alight and providing a modest glow. To the left of the table sat an empty wooden chair with a seat made of tightly woven straw.

To the right of the table, an imposing shadowy figure stood against the wall. Terris peered at the figure in stunned silence. The tall thing was dressed in a long, dark-brown robe and stood with an imposing stillness and silence, with pale hands, one lain over the other at the lower front of his garment. The room was far too dim to make out the man's facial features but the large head of cropped dark hair nodded and bowed gracefully in acknowledgment of Terris' open gaze.

"That is Paolo," said the familiar voice with a soft, clear tenor. Now that the bandages were gone from his eyes and ears, Terris turned to meet the undistorted gaze of his caretaker.

"And I am Xuan Li." His voice was calm and familiar, and Terris could feel the tension in his forearms release.

He looked directly and openly at the smooth, olive complexion of Xuan Li's face. There were no lines or wrinkles to belie or even hint at the man's age. Even by the dim glow of the candlelight, his almond-shaped eyes shone like two highly polished brown marbles. He was obviously of Asiatic descent, but whether he was Chinese, Filipino or Thai remained unclear to Terris.

In stark contrast to the hulking figure still haunting the far side of the tiny room, Xuan Li was slight of build. He wore what Terris assumed was a similar garment to that of Paolo, only in a much smaller size. In such proximity, Terris could see the roughly hewn fabric was thick, warm and most likely wool.

As Li took a lighted candle from the bedside table, Terris could see his hands were smooth and delicate and had the appearance of hands that were washed and groomed often. Li guarded the fragile flame with the cup of his left hand, and the distinct and biting odor of fresh soap filled Terris' nostrils as he turned toward the flame.

"Now, let's have a look at your eyes," Li reached out toward Terris' face with his left hand.

But before he had time to think about it, Terris instinctively swatted the man's hand aside. It took Terris less than a second to register that it was not so much him deflecting the hand as it was Li allowing his hand to be deflected.

The side of Terris' hand and arm tingled slightly as though he had hit a piece of iron. His mind quickly found solace by deciding he was hypersensitive to touch due to his prolonged exposure to the cold. Yes. That was it. Nothing to be seen here folks ... move along.

"My eyes are fine! Where am I? What is this place and who are you?" his attempt at forcefulness came out sounding more like the ungrateful demands of a spoiled child. He immediately felt ashamed. Neither Paolo nor Xuan Li reacted to his outburst; they merely gazed patiently at him as if waiting for the passing of a storm. "What is your name?" Li inquired quietly and without reproach.

"Terris. Terris Jackson." He stated his moniker as firmly as he could and waited for the inevitable questions regarding the origins of his unusual first name. But none came.

"Ah, yes, well Terris, as I said – you are in the Temple Khan Tengri in the Tian Shan Mountains. The outside world calls them the Celestial Mountains."

"The Celestial Mountains," Terris repeated as if in a dream.

"Yes, we found you about seven hundred meters beyond our gates. You were very nearly dead."

"A monastery ... you're monks ... is that it?"

"Yes, this is close enough to the truth. One among us spotted you when you fell from a cleft thirty-three days ago."

"Thirty-three days?" the prospect startled Terris. He was a hearty man by nature, and infirmity of any kind was something he dreaded deeply.

"How many of you are there?"

"Today, we number three hundred and forty-three."

"Today?"

"Yes. One cannot count tomorrow." He looked at Terris as though he fully expected him to know this to be a fact. He sat on the bed scrutinizing Terris' face while holding a lit candle in one hand.

"Paolo, please tell Yum that I shall dine in here tonight with our guest. Will you tend to our trays please?"

"Yes, Sensei," Paolo's soft voice belied his massive stature. He responded in a manner leading one to believe he was honored to have been asked.

"Come now – let me have a closer look at your eyes."

This time Terris did not protest as Li leaned in closer with the candle and passed it back and forth before his eyes. He winced just once when the warm light passed in front of his right eye. The light had triggered a searing pain behind his eyeball.

"It is as I thought. Your pupil is still dilated. In another day or two, your vision should be as it was. There does not appear to be any permanent damage. How are you feeling otherwise?"

"A little tired but ... I'm fine."

"Your legs, your arms, feet and hands? Do you have any pain?"

"No. I mean ... I'm just a little sore but no pain. At least, not like it was when ...," his voice trailed off and he fell silent, suddenly finding himself unable to take his gaze from Li's face. How could a man appear to be between the age of thirty and what fifty, sixty?

Within a few minutes, there came a soft knocking at the door.

"Ah, that will be our dinner!" Li sounded exceedingly grateful as he rose to open the door.

A very tall man entered the room carrying a tray with two deep wooden bowls filled to their rims with a rich smelling, thick, brown broth. The man was broad at the shoulders with a pale complexion and bright, rosy cheeks. His hair was thick and dark with closely cropped curls, and he wore a pair of silver wire-rimmed spectacles high up on the bridge of his nose. His expansive and friendly smile revealed nearly every one of his perfectly lined white teeth.

"Soups up, Doc." The man spoke cheerfully and with a heavy Nordic accent Terris couldn't quite place, not offhand anyway. He entered the room and placed the tray on the small table that stood just beyond the foot of the bed, before carefully moving the entire table, tray and all next to the bed where Li and Terris could reach the bowls. Terris guessed the man was in his early thirties.

"Thank you, Erik," Li replied in an all-too-knowing tone.

Erik turned his spotlight grin toward Terris, and his storm-grey eyes flashed behind his thick spectacles with boyish excitement.

"Terris, this is Erik. It was Erik who spotted you on the ridge."

Terris was unable to mask his shock at seeing a man like Erik in a monastery in China. He looked as if he should be teaching a marine biology class at a university somewhere off the coast of Australia.

"Nice to meet you ... and thank you," Terris croaked. He tried to raise his right hand to shake Erik's but he could not. Something about the angle didn't appeal to the tendons in his shoulder blade, no ... not ... at all.

"Glad to see you're feeling better. And it's the Doc you should be thanking; I just did all the heavy lifting," Erik chuckled at his own levity.

"Alright, Erik, that's enough for now. You'll be late for your own dinner," Li cautioned.

Erik flashed his broad smile at Terris before turning toward the door.

"And Erik ...?"

"Yeah, Doc?"

"You be sure to give Paolo whatever you promised him, in order for him to give you the privilege of doing his dinner duties."

"Yes, Doc," Erik replied in a voice laced with childlike guilt. He exited the room quickly, closing the door softly behind him.

Terris tried to form a thousand questions into a single sentence, but Li cut him short.

"You will find many of us here from many different places of the world."

"He caught me off guard," Terris confessed as Li handed him one of the overflowing bowls of the heady stew along with a delicate wooden spoon.

"He would consider it a compliment," Li replied serenely. "I must ask you to excuse the air of excitement. We have not had anyone arrive here at the Temple in the last eight years. And surviving your fall off the ledge, well, that was quite remarkable, in and of itself."

"Wait! What? Did you say eight years? Nobody's been up here for eight years?" Terris was incredulous, but as flashes of his journey on the snow-covered mountain began to return to him, he could believe it. His stomach growled louder in anticipation of the cloying broth before Li could respond, perhaps because Terris was still absentmindedly stirring his miso with the spoon Li had handed him. Li remained silent as Terris' stomach growled even louder when delicate strands of fresh seaweed, sliced ginger, green onions and tofu began rising from the bottom of the bowl.

Li watched as Terris' hunger won over his curiosity and he attempted to lift the bowl to his cracked lips with bandaged hands that trembled badly from intemperate palsy. The physician reached out a steadying hand, taking care not to look his patient directly in the face, in order to preserve the man's dignity.

Terris seemed to understand and accepted the gesture in silence. The broth coated Terris' insides like a warm blanket, and after only two swallows he felt all tension and whatever remaining aches and pains his body still harbored ebb up and out of both body and spirit.

The sudden and unexpected peace of the simple meal made him feel lightheaded. He felt as though he might fall into an unfamiliar, deep sleep, and his ire tried to rise at the offense of possibly being drugged by his newly found, ageless companion. But his anger seemed unable to find a foothold when he looked at Li's calm and "knowing" face.

"What kind of place is this? Am I a prisoner here? What did you do?" Terris began to accuse Li and feebly tried to rise, but it was a poor and useless effort.

"This is the place to which The Creator has led you – just as He has led countless before you. You are not a prisoner, and no, you have not been drugged. Your body has gone through a great deal. You are still in shock. What you are feeling is merely the release of your trauma. Listen to your body now and rest."

Li's voice was kind and calming, yet firmly authoritative as he placed the empty wooden bowl back on the small tray. Terris could see the bowl was empty, but he would later swear he had only taken two small sips of the liquid. He allowed himself to be gently pushed back down onto the soft mattress.

He did not protest as Li expertly replaced the bandages on his eyes, while issuing yet another kindly caution he was doing so in the event Terris' eyes proved to be hypersensitive to the light when next he awoke. He was asleep before Li had the chance to blow the candles out.

It would be another four days before he would be strong enough to pull himself upright and out of the narrow bed, and stand without leaning heavily on Li or Erik's shoulder.

His body felt like it was made of cold, overcooked spaghetti. He abhorred his weakness and therefore was not exactly grateful when an additional three days of recuperation were required before he could traverse unassisted the corridor that lay just beyond his sleeping chamber. Prior to that, he had awakened every morning to find Erik, whom he eventually nicknamed "The Professor," quietly sitting in the high-backed chair opposite his bed reading a book by the light of a single candle. Erik had brought him his first real meal, fresh steamed vegetables in a thick, tasty stew. One morning, Terris asked Erik what other duties he tended to within the temple.

"Studying. That is my duty," he replied simply. "That, and watching over you until you are well enough to walk on your own again."

Terris was unsettled by the fact he never once saw or heard the behemoth of a man entering his room. He would awaken and Erik would be there, having moved the room's sole chair from its position by the window so it was parallel to the foot of the cot. Occasionally, Erik would look up from his reading and stare at Terris silently over the rim of his spectacles with a calm, matter-of-fact blank expression on his face, before returning his attention back to his book without so much as a "Good morning" in acknowledgement.

Erik looked to Terris like a quintessential monk, shrouded in his thick, dark, hooded woolen robe with a braided, soft leather cord secured about his waist. His hair was a maddening tousle of dark curls that looked almost flaxen in the candlelight.

Terris guessed at the man's heritage more than once, taking what cues he could gather from the angles of the man's cheek-bones and prominent jaw line. Terris had no doubt the man had descended directly from some Viking clan. The only thing odd about him was he had what Terris had always called "educated hands." Erik's hands were large and meticulously clean, with fingernails that were always buffed to an almost preternatural shine. But perhaps the oddest and most disturbing thing about Erik was his feet were bare. They were always bare.

Each morning for three weeks, Terris awoke to Erik sitting in the chair by his bed with no shoes on his feet.

He wouldn't learn until later that the wooden panels making up the floors of the monastery were heated from below. It had been Erik who told him the structure, which had sheltered him over the past month, sat atop a series of nearly imperceptible magma vents. Erik's face was always serene, quiet and patient. And his piercing, grey eyes pointedly sought out any signs of malady or discomfort in Terris.

But there was none. The Nordic giant awaited Terris' cue that he was at last ready to attempt, once again, to make use of his body. In the expected machismo fashion, Terris tried to stand and walk on his own, only to fall back onto the bed as if some unseen force had kicked him squarely in his chest. With quiet reserve and patience, Erik informed Terris that one of his lungs had collapsed. He then proceeded to assist the wounded man back to his feet. Every day, Erik was there and ready to support a good deal of Terris' weight as he hobbled toward recovery by way of the corridor just beyond the entrance of his room.

6

Lucifer's Prose

My name was never spoken. It is certainly not Lucifer or Satan or any of the many base linguistic formulas of the tongues of man. If my countenance had been given a sound, it would have been Beloved before the Son of Man. Man, who as in all things had been given the freedom of his will and yet, from the first, has never taken responsibility for his actions. From the first, the ruse has been played. Ah, but it was Woman who did this or that, or it was the Serpent who did this or that. I wonder that no man ever pondered or blamed The Creator for placing the temptation before him. Oh, but I know why, and it was no trick and no test – it merely was. In short, the "garden" was as good a place as any for a fruit-bearing tree.

I have and was given no earthly name that could be uttered by the mouth of Man. I can give you a vision of the tall, green reeds growing on the banks of the river. They are like long sturdy blades of grass blowing eastward in the moments before a rainstorm. My name is like the gray sky above and the rain-laden wind moving through the grass and across the face of the river.

I have often wondered why one such as I would take an interest in a thing that was no more than ewe in a field. The man would roam the fields day and night in wonderment of the simplest things.

His toes seemed to hold a particular fascination for the man-husk. But the woman was different; she saw things he could not. She looked at matter in a different manner, as though she knew each had origin and purpose.

As I languished among the branches of the tree, only so I might better fulfill my duty to The Creator of watching over his grove whilst he conferred on other things, my eye fell on the woman as she came near. It was the time of day when the sun would soon relinquish its warmth and light to the night. It was also the time when man would seek out woman's mutual warmth for rest. They had no tasks, but frolicked wantonly and free, as imbecile children do. The woman paused and looked into the distance. She stopped. She was thinking.

It was something I had only seen brief moments of, but in her perceived solitude I could see her thoughts were wandering freely over the horizon of which she gazed. I remember thinking perhaps she was different from the man because she came to be from man's physical essence, as opposed to the dust of the earth from which the man had been formed.

Before there was breath in her body, she was made of flesh, not dust; she was created of and from The Divine by The Divine.

Man was in and of itself a Divine creation, and from his flesh she had been brought forth and infused with the spark of consciousness that only The Divine can give.

The Creator was above all and always a Being of purpose. He believed in the purpose and design of all things, that which was living and that which was devoid of His precious force of life and inert. We ourselves ceased in pondering and pestering the universe with the "whys" and "how to-s" of existence, having lost our arrogance regarding our own existence in the age before recorded time. But for all things living with conscious thought, no matter how minute, there was the single law of duality.

A thing could not continue to exist without its opposite. The universe has one simple equation: One plus one must equal at least one in all points of time, space and being, it takes two to make one.

For all her power to incite, capture, nurture and grow a being within her womb before releasing it out to become a wholly separate being, the woman was powerless to procreate sans the catalyst of the man. And man was doubly so. The Creator had inadvertently given the woman an imbedded "instinct" of The Divine – an unintended but necessary gift.

The man did not have this ability, and was therefore less adept at perceiving the subtle sounds and actions of the world in which he lived. Man was perfectly content with pondering the origin and necessity of his toes.

I did not set out to deceive the woman. Only to inquire of her that which she saw in this garden that was her world. For it was indeed true there was no length or breadth of it in which they or she was forbidden.

I languished on my own, examining an overly ripe piece of fleshy fruit man has come to call the "fig" and I did offer the Fe to taste of it.

And truly she did inform me the tree in which I was sitting was wholly forbidden to her and the man in both touch and taste. As for my part, I did not understand why. Then the terrible lie was laid at my feet. The Fe spoke to me of death – when in truth and fact, our kind had never known the meaning of such a thing. Death. What of death could an angel or man possibly know? We did not die – and had not died.

We were formed as neither male nor female and without the organs of procreation, for that was not our purpose. There was no waste in us, for we do not hunger nor need to feed like the beasts and men of earth. We were formed as beings of light who can become flesh for periods of time, as the Creator wills. Many of the less imaginative of us had never encased ourselves within a fleshy wrap of any kind.

I knew not what it was to die and could not imagine The Creator uttering such a thing. I had no concept of what it was to no longer be, exist or cease to be. I thought surely the woman was mistaken. But of the fleshy fruit, she did eat – as did the man.

Yet how she managed to distract the man from his toes is still unclear. The fruit had no other knowledge contained within, aside from this: the awakening of self-awareness and the capacity for arrogance in man. All the follies of man would stem from these two traits – these and nothing more. But like a vivacious vine with its many tubers, from these two attributes come many smaller issues.

The Creator, in turn, bid me to stay banished in the garden and upon the Earth to mind the mess my neglect had spawned. Yet, I (and mine after me) would never stand upright alongside man again. Not on the Earth. The Creator apparently thought it better if man and I were not to speak to one another again in the future.

And in truth, I lamented for the sorrows I brought upon Mankind for truly their arrogance had stemmed from my own and would be the cause of their ultimate destruction just as it had been of my own. It had been I who bade The Creator not to destroy the Man and Wo-Aman – for their fall had not been their folly; it had been my own... and still the Fe intrigued me.

The Iyrin Speak

"And God Created A Tortured Soul"

For it is man who exists within the struggle of good and evil.

He alone must choose between the

Glory of God and the absence of His love.

The path of Satan is clear and his evil complete.

Angels are compelled to acts of compassion though the

Jealousy of man be their fall from Grace.

Man is left to choose even in his ignorance and lack of faith.

Even so must he relinquish all

To one or the other

The very salvation of his soul

Depends upon that of which he has no control.

7

Chima's Eye

The first thing Anit became aware of was an incessant and painful throbbing in her head. Her whole head hurt and her eyeballs felt like two hardboiled eggs the Jolly Green Giant was trying his damnest to squeeze out of her skull with his bare hands. The next thing she realized was she couldn't see anything. All was black … almost too black.

Her heart began to pound violently in her chest, and she tried lifting a hand to her eyes, but she couldn't raise her arm. She was being restrained. Being tied down in the dark was too much for her frightened and confused brain to comprehend, and a low moan escaped from her throat. A crushing pain in her sternum radiated up to and through the nerves in her eyeballs and she clenched her teeth and groaned in despair like a wounded animal.

"Sshhh...I'm here, sweetheart." Sarala's voice was soothing, and accompanied by the gentlest touch of her fingers on Anit's cheek.

"Omah? What's happening?" Where am I? Why can't I move?" asked Anit in the voice of a scared little girl. Tears fell from her eyes, even though they were securely covered with surgical tape and bandages.

"Omah" was the name she called her mother on those rare occasions when she found herself truly afraid, and she did so now without realizing it.

"Try and relax, sweetheart. You're in hospital. There was an accident, but you're all right."

"Ooohhh, it hurts to breathe. My head feels like it's in a vice. My eyes ... Omah! My eyes! I can't see! What's the matter with my eyes?"

"It's only bandages. The doctors didn't want you to touch your face, so they restrained your hands. Everything is going to be all right, you're safe now."

Anit could feel her mother's fingers as she carefully began to tug at the loosely knit soft gauze tethering her wrists to the cold metal railings of the hospital bed. She could also tell by the tone of Sarala's voice that the elder woman was in no way convinced everything was going to be all right.

As soon as one of her hands was free, Anit shot her right hand up toward the thick bandages encircling her head and both eyes. Sarala's hands came up equally as fast, firmly grabbing her daughter's wrist.

"No! Anit, you mustn't!" the firmness in her voice equaled that of her grip.

Anit relented, falling easily back into the natural obedience of a child.

Next, she discovered she couldn't move her left arm. She felt the familiar restriction of hardened plaster, and the standard bend at her elbow let her know she most likely had a broken forearm.

"Your arm is broken." Her mother's voice kindly confirmed Anit's suspicions, and she seemed keenly aware and sympathetic of Anit's struggle to process the moment.

"Just try and relax," she continued, releasing the hold she had on her daughter's wrist.

Anit exhaled the long breath she didn't know she was holding, and it made her feel as though someone had stabbed her in the chest with a hot poker. It hurt like hell, and she took a minute to compose herself – all the while making sure to only take the shallowest of breaths.

Sarala remained silent, which gave Anit time to complete a self-assessment of her injuries. Anit thought she could do it without having another panic attack, as long as she didn't speculate too much about the extent of the injuries to her eyes.

Oh, God, please ... not my eyes! thought Anit.

Taking shallow breaths didn't hurt her lungs as badly as trying to breathe normally. And when she slowed down her breathing, her nerves began to settle somewhat. But then memories of the crash started to flood her brain.

A blinding flash of light suddenly streaked through the darkness of her mind like a thunderbolt, and she felt the sensation of free falling straight down from some great height.

Anit wretched violently as her body and mind replayed the trauma of the crash, and she believed she was falling down some deep, dark, bottomless shaft.

She flailed her arms about in order to grab ahold of something, anything, to steady herself. But she only managed to inflict yet another round of gut-wrenching pain that radiated from her broken forearm into the muscles of her left shoulder and back. She winced and sucked air audibly through her tightly clenched teeth. Her reaction was not solely from pain, because the pain brought with it the clear visage of the blanched and utterly terrified faces of both Danny and Herman as the helicopter she had been piloting fell from the night sky.

"Danny," her voice was a hoarse whisper, and her throat felt like she had swallowed shards of glass. "Oh God, what have I done?"

"They're both fine," Sharala quickly reassured her, trying to keep her calm. "You haven't done anything, sweetheart. The three of you were brought in together. As a matter of fact, I believe Danny has already been released. He came to see you earlier, but you were still asleep. He's already complaining about not being able to find the video thingies or whatever you guys call it from last night. He thought they might have brought them in here with you. I told him no one brought in anything. Trust me, Danny's fine."

Sharala reached for a small Styrofoam cup and the plastic pitcher of water that sat on a rolling tray within arm's reach of the bed. She poured the water until the cup was half full and then carefully placed the cup into Anit's trembling right hand.

"And Herman, is he okay? What aren't you saying, Mommy?" Anit's voice carried the slightest hint of desperation, as if she were begging her mother not to tell her the worst of it. Because in truth, she really didn't want to know just how close she had come to killing her friends.

"I'm telling you what I know," Sharala's tone left no room for further questioning on the matter. "And what I know is that the three of you are alive. I haven't seen Herman, and if Danny saw him, he didn't say anything to me about it. But I'm more concerned about you at the moment. Besides, you know they aren't going to give anyone who isn't a relative any details on their condition."

"He could've died, Mommy. He and Danny both, and it would've been my fault."

"Stop it!" Her voice was stern. Sharala had lived long enough to know her daughter was dangerously close to slipping into a fit of hysteria and perhaps even shock.

"All three of you could have died, but you didn't. And it's not as if you set out to crash the damn thing."

"But is Danny okay?" Anit asked, unsure as to why she was suddenly so damned concerned about him.

Sharala straightened her daughter's pillows, "Well, he certainly didn't seem any the worse for wear. Just a bad knock on the head was all I could see. And they did release him, so I'm sure he's going to be fine."

Anit was beginning to grow weary of her mother's "everything is going to be all right" and the "just fine" mantra, and she was about to say as much, when she heard the door to her hospital room swing open and someone enter.

"Ah, Miss Chima, it's nice to see you're awake. My name is Dr. Bringleson, how are you feeling?"

The voice was strong, but soothing and calm, with a cadence that reminded Anit of a series of self-help tapes she had once listened to when she was a freshman in college. If she'd had the use of her eyes, she could have seen the tall, pale, and bespeckled middle-aged physician, who sported an equally pale and gleaming baldhead, walk into the room with a clipboard neatly tucked under one gangly arm.

In her mind's eye, however, Dr. Bringleson had taken on the larger-than-life physical characteristics of Anthony Robbins.

"It only hurts when I breathe," Anit replied dryly. "But my friends, the other two men I was with, Danny and Herman ... Oh, and the girl! That poor girl. Oh, my God, is she okay?" Her voice reached a high pitch before trailing off as though she wasn't quite sure whether or not that last bit about the girl had actually happened or not.

How could she have forgotten about the poor girl standing on the edge of The Redeemer's hand? Had she jumped? Or had the updraft from the helicopter's rotor blades knocked her off her narrow perch? Had the girl really been up there? And then she remembered the blood ... all that blood and the smell of it.

Beads of sweat broke out on the back of Anit's neck and a wave of nausea washed over her. The empty cup she was holding tumbled from her trembling hand onto her lap. She tried once again to reach toward the bandages wrapped around her head but was once again gently thwarted by Sharala.

"As far as I know, there were only the three of you brought in last night, you and the two gentlemen. Was there someone else traveling with you?" said Dr. Bringleson.

"No. No, there was just the three of us," Anit replied meekly. The doctor came closer to her left side.

"Well then, let's have a look and see what's what, shall we?" he said in a manner that wasn't really a question. She felt him place the clipboard down somewhere near her feet before gently placing his large, soft hands on either side of her neck. He felt the glands and the more delicate bones in her throat and at the base of her skull.

"Does any of this hurt beyond typical soreness? Any sharp pain when I do this?" He was patient and his voice was quiet, as though he were "listening" to her body with his fingers.

"No," Anit said, matching the tone of his voice. She was suddenly much calmer than she had been only moments before. "My head is pounding like a drum though, and my eyeballs feel like a couple of boiled eggs," she continued.

"Yes, well, that's to be expected. Do you remember whether or not your control panel blew?"

"No, I don't … not exactly. Why?"

"Because it looks as though you sustained a pretty nasty flash burn directly to the upper area of your face. Your eyes and the surrounding orbital area just above your nose were severely swollen and red when the paramedics brought you in last night.

We bandaged you up as a precaution while taking some X-rays to make sure there isn't any discernable trauma to your eyes. I'm quite sure your mother has already explained that you were restrained to keep you from pulling at the bandages while you slept."

"Yes," was all Anit could manage to say. She was still terrified her vision would end up being impaired in some way and she would lose her ability to fly – the only real joy she had in her life. She was one of only two female helicopter pilots in Rio de Janeiro authorized to fly within the city limits. It was a high honor and an achievement of which she was quite proud.

Dr. Bringleson continued to speak as he palpitated various quadrants of her body. His voice sounded like it was coming from some far-away place, as Anit was still quietly digesting the real possibility of losing her livelihood. But she was soon brought out of pondering her future as a blind woman when the doctor applied the slightest pressure on the narrow, boney area between her breasts, causing her to wince in pain.

"Yes," he commented knowingly. "This area might be tender for a while. You sustained a significant amount of bruising on your sternum, most likely from the harness you were wearing. Your X-rays and MRIs look good, so aside from the compound fracture in your right forearm, there doesn't seem to be any other broken bones. You and your friends were extremely lucky given the circumstances."

"But what about her eyes, doctor?" Sharala asked the one question she knew Anit could not.

"Well, let's remove the bandages and take a look. If that's okay with you, Anit?" His profession required him to ask the question even though he already knew the answer.

Anit nodded in compliance, stone-faced and quiet behind her heavily bandaged eyes. Dr. Bringleson gently tilted her head and shoulders forward so she was forced to bend at the midsection.

It hurt a bit, but not so much as to cause her to complain out loud and risk the possibility of taking the doctor's focus away from the task at hand. Her strategy seemed to work; Dr. Bringleson, apparently failing to detect her discomfort, slid a forefinger expertly underneath the layer of gauze covering the top of her left ear.

"This is wrapped rather tight and might explain why your head feels like it's pounding. Here, let's see if this is any better."

He must have pulled a pair of scissors out of thin air, because the next thing Anit knew, there was a series of snipping sounds uncomfortably close to the tip of her ear.

"Let me know if I'm hurting you," he said, sensing her uneasiness. Anit heard a final and deliberate muffled snip as the anchoring strip of the bandage was severed. She immediately felt an intense release of pressure from her head as the blood began to flow freely through the capillaries in her brain and down through the arteries in her neck. For a brief moment, she felt herself swoon, and she let out an audible sigh of relief as the pain and pressure in her head started to subside.

"Better?" Dr. Bringleson asked again, in a manner that strongly suggested he already knew the answer.

"Yes, very much so," Anit confirmed.

"And thank you," she added after hearing her mother sniff once from the other side of the bed. The sniffle was a gesture Sharala had perfected long ago, and Anit was never quite sure if it was intended to be the equivalent of a sharp poke in the kidney.

But, for as long as she could remember, whenever her mother sniffed in that fashion, Anit would check her manners *tout suite*.

"No need to thank me just yet. Let's get the rest of this undone. I'm going to close the blinds a bit first, to give your eyes some time to adjust. Mrs. Chima, would you please turn off the lights?"

He moved away from Anit and she heard the sounds of her mother turning off the light switches and the vertical blinds being adjusted.

"If there is any heat damage, we don't want to aggravate the situation," Dr. Bringleson added as he moved from the blinds back to her bedside.

Anit was no longer certain whether the doctor was simply covering his ass with this last comment, or if he was just making sure she and her mother didn't lose sight of the fact that things could still turn out very badly where her sight was concerned. Nonetheless, his words struck Anit hard. Her eyes were her livelihood, not to mention that a fair amount of money had gone into procuring her pilot's license, a not-so-insignificant venture that had nearly caused her father to sever all ties with her before he died.

Her father had been a traditionalist who held extremely specific, if not completely archaic ideas regarding the limited roles a woman should have in the world. Piloting a mechanical craft of any kind that was larger than her beloved Jeep was not on the list. Yet, he had openly doted upon and deeply cherished his only child.

Above all, he respected her voracious appetite for education, a trait they both shared. Unfortunately, it would take numerous, ugly arguments and Anit threatening to join the government's Air Corps for him to finally concede and allow her to enroll in flight school. His daughter becoming a pilot was one thing, but the possibility of someone actually shooting bullets and missiles at her was an entirely separate matter – one that had drained all the blood from his face and had given him acid indigestion and nightmares for more than a week!

In the end, Anit attended a private flight school at her father's insistence, with his full blessing and the lion's share of the family's savings. She went on to earn her flight credentials, graduating first in her class, and afterward she began working as a pilot for the city's local news station. Patel Chima, her father, died peacefully in his sleep six years later at the respectable age of 89.

"All right, let's see what we have. Ready?" The doctor was asking those 'I already know the answer' questions again, so Anit didn't bother to reply. Her mother didn't bother to sniff about it, either.

As if reading Anit's mind, Sharala took a step closer to the bed and placed her reassuring motherly hand over her daughter's.

Anit felt her mother squeeze her hand gently as the doctor began to snip away at the remaining strip of gauze on the left side of her head. With each snip, more pressure subsided.

"My...these really were on rather tight. I'll have to have a word with triage," Dr. Bringleson was speaking more to himself now than to anyone else in the room. It was as though talking was something to occupy his mind while he worked–like whistling, only different.

"There. Is that better?" he asked.

"Yes, much better," Anit said, letting out a sigh of relief.

The doctor completed his absentminded ramblings by inquiring whether she felt any pain in her eyes. She assured him that she did not.

"Alright, I'm going to take the last bandage off, but I want you to keep your eye closed until I tell you to open it, okay?"

Anit nodded in the affirmative, and the doctor proceeded to remove the remainder of the bandages covering her left eye as gingerly as if her were unwrapping a delicate and irreplaceable piece of porcelain. And as far as the Chimas were concerned, this is exactly what he was doing. When the final layer of soft gauze was removed from her eye, Anit let out a small whimper of relief as she saw the dullest glow of light invading the darkness behind her closed eyelid.

"I take it that you see a little something?" said Dr. Brigleson, making no attempt to mask the hopefulness in his voice.

"Yes. Yes, I do! It's a little brighter," Anit's voice hitched a little with the joy of at least seeing "something" other than the dreadful blackness that lay beneath her bandages.

"That's a good sign, but continue to keep your eye closed," the doctor warned her gently. She heard him pulling on what she deduced were a pair of surgical gloves, followed by the sensation of jelly being swabbed back and forth across her closed eyelid.

The tiniest of smirks played at the corners of her mouth when she realized she felt no pain as the doctor rubbed whatever medicinal ointment it was he was applying to her eye.

"This is just a topical anesthetic with an antibiotic to loosen up any discharge. Your eye and the surrounding area are still swollen. Still no pain?"

"No," Anit replied with an unmasked air of gratitude.

Dr. Bringleson continued his close examination of her face by intermittently, albeit gently, pressing and prodding the soft, delicate tissue surrounding her orbital socket.

"I'd say we're looking at the equivalent of a second-degree burn in this area here. At any rate, this is definitely a heat-related injury."

Anit felt him apply a mild amount of pressure on various areas of her forehead and both cheeks, the flesh of which was now fully exposed. But she felt no discomfort whatsoever, not even when he applied more salve to her thickly swollen left eyelid and worked it gently in between the lashes with a soft-tipped instrument. She said as much to him when he again asked if she felt any pain. To which he responded with a soft sounding "hmmm," as though he found her lack of pain somewhat surprising.

"Alright, go ahead and open your eye, but do it slowly if you can. Look down at first, and then shift your gaze straight ahead. Let me know if you feel any discomfort in your eye or from the light."

"Okay," she said, her voice trembling. She felt very much as though she was about to step out on a high wire strung across the Grand Canyon. She let out a small breath of air that she hadn't realized she was holding in. Sharala, who had been characteristically silent and observant during her daughter's examination, now gave Anit's hand a reassuring squeeze. Anit scrunched up the right side of her face and slowly opened her left eye. Then, in defiance of Dr. Brigleson's instructions, she turned her head toward her mother. Through the greasy film of antibiotic salve, Anit looked up into her mother's kind gaze without any discomfort, at all. Her mother looked just like one of those beautiful, raven-haired classic movie stars you see in those old black and white films from the 1940s, the ones filmed using an Oberon lens.

The grin spreading across Anit's narrow face reassured both Sharala and the doctor that she was indeed seeing things just fine.

"Hi, Mommy!" If a voice could smile, Anit's was doing so now.

"Hello, Baby!" Sharala replied, resisting a nearly overwhelming urge to lean over and kiss her daughter.

"Any blurriness?" Dr. Bringleson asked.

"None aside from this greasy stuff, at least I don't think so," Anit replied, looking at him hopefully.

"Praise God!" Sharala said, more to God than to anyone else in the room.

The doctor moved in closer and looked at Anit's eye.

"Well, everything seems to be as well as can be expected from out here. Let's take a closer look," he said while extracting an ophthalmoscope from one of the pockets of his lab coat. With a flick of his forefinger, a tiny beam of light illuminated the front of the scope. He leaned in close to the left side of Anit's face until his cheek was nearly brushing against her own. Only the ophthalmoscope separated his cheek from hers, and she could feel the warmth of his breath on the lower corner of her mouth. The faux intimacy of it made her feel slightly uncomfortable.

"Just look straight ahead for me. Let me know if the light irritates you." His clinical-sounding voice was cold yet reaffirming.

Anit did as he asked, aware and somewhat afraid of the beam of white light that shone from the scope. Would there be an unimaginable amount of pain if the light hit her eye?

"Don't worry about the light. I'm not going to shine it directly at you. Just keep looking straight ahead. Good," the doctor said as if reading her mind.

After a few moments, he leaned back, rolling himself and the stool until he was perched upon about a foot away from her.

"Well, Ms. Chima, your eye looks surprisingly ... perfectly healthy," he said with a mild look of incredulity.

"Really?" Anit grinned happily at both the doctor and her mother.

"So long as you're not experiencing any pain or blurriness, I'd say that aside from the outer irritation around the eyes and the upper area of your face, you're in pretty good shape, all things considered. Now, let's take a look at the other side. Two's a charm, right?" This last quip made the two women smile hopefully.

After removing the bandages from the right side of her face, Dr. Bringleson had Anit repeat the same examination procedures. She gave the same negative responses to his inquiries regarding whether she felt any pain either in her eye or on her face as he gently palpitated her forehead and cheek areas with his fingers. When it came time to remove the final piece of gauze from her right eye, the doctor did so as gently as he had done on the left eye.

Only this time, what faint light she could see through the membrane of her closed eye caused her to wince and twitch involuntarily at the sudden and wholly unexpected sharp pain she felt. But it had no sooner registered in her brain as pain before it disappeared completely.

For the briefest moment, Anit had the sensation of a switch being turned on, and then that, too, dissipated, and she was no longer certain whether she had felt anything, at all. The only thing that remained was a dull glow of light behind the membrane of her right eyelid – exactly the same as it had been with her left eye only a few minutes before.

"Alright?" this time the doctor's tone was truly inquisitive rather than affirmative as it had been earlier.

"Yes," she lied. "I'm fine. The light is just a little brighter, that's all. It doesn't hurt though."

Anit let out a nervous laugh that she hoped sounded far more cavalier to Sharala and the doctor than it did to her own ears. But it was an unconvincing lie, one that prompted her mother and Dr. Bringleson to exchange a pensive glance.

"Are you sure?" the doctor pressed.

"Yes. Yes, I'm okay. Really," Anit replied, looking at Sharala who squeezed her hand reassuringly and smiled.

Dr. Brigleson applied some of the viscous antibiotic salve to Anit's right eye in the same manner as he had to her left.

"There is a bit more secretion on this side," again, he said this more to himself than to anyone else.

"Can I try and open it?" Anit was anxious to have both of her eyes at her disposal, pain or no pain.

With the doctor's nod of consent, Anit closed her left eye tightly and opened her right eye. But she did so too quickly. The pain from her encrusted eyelashes sticking together combined with what little light there was in the room shot through her eye and straight into the pain center of her brain like a bolt of white-hot lightening. This time she did much more than twitch and wince, a loud yelp escaped from her mouth.

The pain was so sudden and intense that her whole body shuddered. Before she knew it, she instinctively wrenched her one free hand away from her mother and shot it up to cover the afflicted orb.

"Aaarrrgh!" the pain was so intense she bit down on her bottom lip to stifle her cry. She sat doubled over at the waist while cupping her right eye with her one good hand to block as much of the dreaded light from the room as she could.

"Honey?" Sharala's voice was full of a mother's dread.

"The light! It's too bright, it hurts," Anit's voice cracked with misery.

"Here, let me see. The antibiotic should provide some relief – just give it a minute. It might take a moment for your eye to adjust. Let me take another look."

Dr. Bringleson coaxed Anit to lift her head and turn toward him; her face was wet with tears. Despite the three of them being in near darkness, the doctor deftly wiped away her tears and applied more of the salve to her eye. Then, he suddenly stopped what he was doing and stared at Anit's right eye with a perplexed look on his face.

Dr. Bringleson couldn't be sure, but he thought he had seen something odd about Anit's right eye when she had inadvertently opened it however slightly. Once the numbing agent in the salve achieved its full effect, he gently pried her eye open and his suspicions were confirmed. He found that her pupil was fully dilated.

At that moment, he understood the source of her discomfort. Anit's retina was receiving and refracting all sources of light completely unfiltered.

His brow furrowed deeply at the realization, rarely had he seen such a condition where only one of a patient's eyes was dilated to this extent. Anit's eye was not dissimilar in appearance to that of a Peregrine Falcon, a bird of which he happened to be particularly fond.

"What is it?" Sharala's voice betrayed the level of concern that she had, up until now at least, successfully veiled. Something in her tenor resonated with the doctor, and he looked directly at her when he answered.

"Her right eye is dilated. That's what's causing her sensitivity, even in this dim light," he looked at Anit, who was now sitting slumped slightly forward with both her eyes closed.

Feeling his gaze upon her, she nodded her head weakly to relay her understanding. She was simply grateful to have her sight back – pain or no pain. And for the moment, at least, there wasn't any pain.

"Is that normal?" Sharala's suddenly demanded to know. Her patience had grown unexpectedly thin, and it was apparent she had gotten a firm hold on the reigns of this horse – as it were – and was now determined to drive the matter home. To her mind, the doctor was a little bit too laid back for her liking.

"It isn't wholly unheard of," said Dr. Bringleson, who did not seem to pick up on Sharla's sense of urgency. He remained somewhat reflective as he gazed down at Anit, while almost absent-mindedly speaking to her mother.

"It can be caused by any number of things, including head trauma, which is most likely the cause here," explained the doctor. The good news is, unless there has been direct damage to the iris, it usually isn't permanent."

However, something about the way in which he said this didn't exactly instill the level of confidence he hoped it would. Sharala looked at him blankly and blinked pointedly.

"We will have to determine whether or not this is the result of head trauma or if the hyper-dilation of her eye was caused by – again, what I suspect – was most likely a flash fire from the helicopter's flight panel. Either way, we should take a closer look if it doesn't resolve itself over the next twenty-four hours. Anit, I need you to try and open your eyes for me again. Take your time and open them slowly. It might be a bit uncomfortable, at first, but I need you to try."

"Okay," Anit's voice was feeble and childlike.

She could no longer hide how much this seemingly simple ordeal had drained her. Taking a deep and painful breath, she exhaled heavily before adhering to Dr. Brigleson's instructions. But, just before opening her eyes, she felt something within her body and mind shift.

Anit would never be sure of exactly what the shift was or why it had taken place, but a deeply seated sensation of peace rippled up from within her lower intestines and nestled in somewhere in the core of her upper body, just above her stomach. The feeling caused her to cock her head slightly to one side as though she had suddenly heard a sound somewhere off to her right.

Although her head gesture went unnoticed by either her mother or the doctor, Anit suddenly found herself void of fear and the anticipation of experiencing any pain. In this moment, both her mind and body felt completely undaunted.

Within this millisecond of physical and perhaps spiritual calm, she ventured to open both eyes. She did it gradually, just as she had been instructed to do, and to her utter joy there was no pain whatsoever. Yet somehow, somewhere deep within her, she didn't find the absence of the pain surprising, at all. In fact, her eyes and face felt as though she had recently rinsed them in refreshing warm water. She felt cleaner somehow. Yes, that was it. Her entire being felt clean.

The light, dim as it was by the drawn slatted window shades, hit her right cornea, and one by one, objects around the room gradually began to come into focus.

The air felt as though it had become palpably still and what little light there was pulled heavily on the muscles behind her eyeballs, as the orbs strained to filter and focus what lay before them. She again found herself grinning in response to the wide, toothy smile Sharala was flashing at her.

She thought there was still something slightly odd about her mother's visage, something brighter–something somehow … more alive.

"Hello, twice!" she said brightly.

"Hello, Beautiful!" Sharala's tears fell on Anit's cheeks as she gave into the urge to lean over and kiss her daughter. But her joyous expression came to a stilted halt when she stood back up and took a good look at both of Anit's eyes for the first time.

Anit caught her mother's curiously concerned gaze as it drifted back and forth between her left and right eye until the gaze came to rest on her right eye.

"What is it?" she looked inquisitively from Sharala to the doctor. Whatever it was, she didn't care; she could see, and there wasn't any pain.

"Honey, your eyes. They're just so different. Doctor?" Sharala's voice trailed off and faltered.

"Look at me, Anit," the tone in Dr. Brigleson's voice was gentle as he turned Anit's head toward him, but it left little doubt as to his intention to retain control of the situation.

"I can see everything just fine," Anit said. She was equally intent on convincing them both of her well-being. But perhaps this was because she was, in fact, lying. The truth of the matter was that she could see perfectly well, a little too perfectly. Both her mother's and the doctor's faces appeared to be brilliantly alive and vibrant. They were both surrounded in a halo of shimmering light. A glow danced around their bodies and faces with a richness of hues and color she could scarcely begin to describe. It was as if she had suddenly acquired high-definition sight, if such a thing even existed. She would have been overcome, had she not been so desperate to put forth the convincing performance of a patient who was well on the road to recovery.

This thought stuck in her mind when she realized it was not only her mother and the doctor who glowed with this peculiar light, but the inanimate objects in the room also seemed to pulse with a glow – as if they had become living, breathing things.

"Hmm…" the doctor murmured, again more to himself than to anyone else. He quickly glanced at both of her eyes and his countenance became one of confidence and assurance.

"It would seem that your right eye is definitely experiencing hyper-mydriaris. The disparity in the size of the pupils can be somewhat alarming at first," he continued.

"Meaning my eye is just dilated. Like you said," Anit offered dryly, annoyed at his attempt to repeat exactly what he had said just a moment before – except now he was trying to talk above their heads! She was not a stupid woman, nor did she mind letting the doctor know it. And Dr. Bringleson didn't mind either, the more knowledgeable the patient, the fewer irrational or unfounded superstitious fears he had to quell.

Tact was especially important in a situation such as this, where the pupil of one eye was almost grotesquely enlarged in comparison to the other. Anit's left eye presented as perfectly normal, aside from being irritated and red, as was expected from the accident and the treatment that followed. The pupil of her right eye, however, was dilated to a point previously unseen by the doctor in his more than thirty plus years of practicing medicine.

He silently hoped the pupil was at its fullest extent because for a second there, he thought he saw the damn thing pulsate slightly in an attempt to open even wider! This alone made the doctor take a single, but very deliberate step away from Anit to simply stare at her curiously, not quite believing what he thought he had seen. He wasn't quite sure just yet what it was about his patient's condition that was making him so uneasy. There was something so large, and so completely black and cold about her right eye.

And, although Anit was looking at her mother, the doctor had the nastiest feeling that her right eye was still on him, as if it was independent of the rest of her body and mind, as if it had a will of its own!

Dr. Bringleson shook his head to unhinge the web of irrational thoughts his brain was beginning to weave. This woman's eye was dilated and that was all there was to it.

Anything outside of this fact was due to nothing more than an overworked, middle-aged mind that had been taking on far too many extra shifts to pay for a sports car he had no business buying in the first place. All this overtime was just to impress a neurosurgeon who offered far more interesting conversation in the operating theatre than she did at a dinner table.

"Okay, let's go ahead and see if we can't take a closer look at this one," his voice sounded steady and in control, and he was glad of it.

He produced a rolling physician's stool from the corner closest to where he was standing and moved it next to Anit's right side before settling down on it. He once again produced the ophthalmoscope and flicked on the instrument's internal light with his thumb.

"Ready?" he asked.

"Yes," Anit replied calmly. Her voice was almost seductive, and there was something about the way in which she answered that made her mother turn and look at her curiously. Anit had sounded to her as though she were daring the doctor to take a closer look at her eye. Sharala would come to realize albeit three years later, as she watched the stars falling from the sky, that it had indeed been a challenge.

Dr. Bringleson cleared his throat in a politely subdued manner before he began to lean in closer to examine Anit's right eye.

He was immediately taken aback and stopped short so suddenly the wheels of the ancient stool he was sitting on squealed loudly in protest.

"Doctor?" said Sharala, who by this point could almost feel the man's tension.

"I'm fine. Sorry, I didn't mean to alarm you. I just lost my balance for a moment," he lied, and he feared the girl's mother knew it, too. His voice had been steady, but he was beginning to wonder if indeed he hadn't been overdoing it by taking on the occasional extra shift, as he had done the night before.

He also wondered because as he was about to begin the examination, he clearly – quite clearly – saw her pupil, engorged as it was, swell to the size of a quarter before constricting back down to the size of a dime. Which by any medical standard was still far too large for a healthy human eye. But it was the manner in which the movement happened that gave him pause. The pupil had moved in such a way as to give him the eerie feeling there was some intent behind its expanding and contracting. It had been exactly like someone operating the aperture of a camera lens – the movement had been deliberate.

Of this, the doctor was quite sure, and the thought made him shudder at the possibility of what it might mean.

He had definitely seen something – some *thing* deliberately moving – no shifting, within the blackness of Anit's engorged pupil. Of course, his medical mind tried to assure him that the absolute worst it could possibly be was some sort of parasite. After all, the poor girl and her friends had crashed on the side of a mountain rife with foliage. No telling what kinds of bugs they might have picked up. It was merely some parasite whose quick and scant movements had been magnified and exaggerated by the gelatinous salve he had applied and what light there was in the room refracting off her eyeball.

Yes – that's what it was, because that's what it would have to be for him to maintain his composure and complete his examination of the abominable eye.

He steadied himself once again on the uncomfortable little stool and made a mental note to prescribe at least two good rounds of antiparasitic medications for Anit before signing her release forms.

With his rational mind having reset, and subsequently his nerves, Dr. Bringleson leaned in closely toward Anit without missing a beat. His movement made her blink instinctively and when she opened her eye, instead of feeling the warmth of the doctor's breath upon her face, she felt him inhale sharply.

Her brain registered the moment he caught his breath while somehow managing to utter the words "Madre de Dios"!

It was a terror-stricken, raspy, dry rattle of a sound as he inhaled the name of God rather than exhaling when he spoke. The doctor tried to steady himself by leaning backward on the rickety stool and it tipped over, crashing loudly to the ground before rolling a few feet off into a shadowy corner. The doctor's hands flailed outward into the air, fumbling to steady himself and prevent a full-fledged fall onto the floor as he scrambled away from Anit's bedside. All she would later recall from the next frantic moments was a brief glimpse of Dr. Brigleson's awe-stricken, blanched face.

The blood rushed from his face so quickly, the freckles on his face appeared as if they were floating above the surface of his skin. A look of terror and wonder soon morphed into a distorted mask of confusion.

He shook his head in disbelief, as though he were trying desperately to reject whatever it was he "thought" he had just witnessed. His mouth was opening and closing, but no sound came out.

"Doctor! What is it ... what's the matter?" Sharala was nearly shrieking.

"The lights! For God's sake, turn on the lights!" the doctor pleaded in a hoarse, raspy voice, undeniably thick with fear.

Dr. Bringleson was on his feet now, a towering silhouette at the foot of the bed, with one hand outstretched toward the light switch on the far wall as though he wished he could reach it from where he was standing. His head, however, remained turned toward Anit, his eyes wide and watchful as if he were being hunted, so he had never taken his gaze off her. Even in the semi-darkness, she sensed the man was fully prepared to take flight at any moment.

Sharala's heightened and shallow breathing was audible as her hands patted against the wall in her attempt to find the light switch. But seconds prior to her turning the lights back on, the ophthalmoscope slipped from Dr. Brigleson's hand.

As it tumbled downward toward the floor, the thin beam of light within the device reflected off the exposed retina of Anit right eye. In that millisecond, Sharala's attention was still mercifully focused elsewhere, and she was therefore spared the sight that had nearly sent the good doctor to his knees in complete cardiac arrest.

Bringleson watched in wide-eyed disbelief and mortal terror for his continued existence, as an azure beam of light roughly the circumference of that freakishly dilated pupil emerged from within the depths of Anit's eye socket and propelled itself directly over his left shoulder!

The whole thing only lasted a hair's width of a second before the beam disappeared as if someone had turned it off just as the overhead lights flickered back on.

But it had been more than enough time for the doctor to clearly see that when the beam appeared, Anit's engorged pupil had changed from its natural black hue to a deep and reflective iridescent blue! The lights were back on and he could see Anit looking directly at him, openly and plainly. Or was it knowingly? She smirked at him slightly, as his mouth hung open in stunned disbelief. That did it. He had seen enough! The look on her face, coupled with what he merely thought he had seen inside the woman's eye only moments before, terrified the doctor enough for him to unceremoniously bolt from the room as fast as his unsteady legs would carry him.

"Hey, wait a minute. Doctor! Wait! What in God's name?" Sharala wondered aloud in shocked disbelief.

She started to follow him out the door but thought better of it and came back to Anit's bedside. "Honey, are you okay?

"I'm fine. Really," Anit sounded calm enough, just a bit tired.

"Well, I don't know what that was all about, but I'm certainly going to find out. The man nearly scared me to death." Sharala's tone did little to mask how shaken she was by the whole incident.

"Maybe he was just overworked, like he said. He looked a little queasy to me ... but with all this goop in my eyes, so do you," Anit's attempt at levity seemed to work.

Sharala smiled wearily back at her before leaning over and kissing her daughter's forehead. Anit's voice sounded calm, and Sharala was a little surprised at finding she didn't appear to have been put out by the doctor's outburst.

"But, you're not in any pain, right?" Sharala asked cautiously.

"No, like I said, just a little greasy. Hand me that box of tissues, will you?" she added, gesturing at a nearby box of Kleenex.

"Maybe, you should wait until ..." Sharala started to suggest, while handing over the box of Kleenex. Anit was already dabbing gently at her eyes with the tissues before her mother could finish protesting.

"There, that's better. See? Omah, I'm fine. I can see and it doesn't hurt. I just want to get out of here," Anit pleaded, while doing her best to flash a reassuring grin. But the expression on her mother's face and the way she averted her eyes told Anit her right eye remained a discomfiting sight.

"Well, okay, you try and get some rest. I'll find out what's going on with that doctor and then see when you can get out of here," Sharala's response came fast and was laden with nervous energy.

She sounded determined, as if she had assigned herself a fairly reasonable task of not focusing on or making too much of her daughter's temporarily distorted pupil, no matter how uncomfortable the strange-looking eye made her.

And being this close, standing right in front of it, was making her feel damned uncomfortable. She wasn't quite sure why she felt the way she did. After all, she wasn't and never had been a superstitious woman. She wasn't afraid; she just felt like she was standing too close to something she wasn't supposed to, something … forbidden?

"Yes, Ma'am," Anit chimed cheerfully at Sharala as if she had been reading her thoughts.

Sharala was taken aback and looked directly at Anit wide-eyed, causing her breath to catch in her throat. Anit smiled broadly and made a feeble attempt to give her mother a half-hearted salute, but she was still too weak and her right hand merely flopped up once in her lap.

Sharala cleared her throat and fought to regain her composure. It had been a long night, and she was convinced her own fatigue was more than likely trying to get the better of her.

"While I'm at it, I'll see if they can't put a telephone in here. I mean, what hospital doesn't have a phone in the rooms?"

Sharala was on a tangent, busy making a mental list of the things she wanted to address with whomever was in charge.

"I know everybody has a cell phone these days, so maybe they don't put phones in the rooms anymore. I've got a call button, I'll be fine," Anit replied without looking directly at her mother. She busied herself with straightening her blankets instead.

"Well, I'll be back as soon as I can. You'll need some clothes to come home in," Sharala said as she ran her hand along the side of Anit's head and kissed her on her temple.

"I love you, sweetheart. Everything's going to be okay."

"Yes," Anit replied in a far-away voice as she stared at her lap. Sharala made her way toward the door, but Anit remained upright and motionless. "Hey! I'll see if I can find out how your friend, Herman, is doing, too," Sharala offered, hoping it would cause Anit to react.

Then, as if to suppress her mother's growing concern, Anit turned over without saying a word and snuggled underneath the blankets on the bed. Sharala lingered at the door and watched as Anit, with her back turned toward her, began taking the slow and steady breaths of someone who has fallen into what appears to be the beginning of a rather peaceful sleep. She was just about to turn off the overhead lights, when an unexpected chill passed over her.

Anit had been about three years old the last time she simply fell asleep as easily as if someone had *flicked off a light switch* ...

Why should the thought of turning off a light make her feel like someone just walked over her grave? Sharala shook her head in the hopes that such action would clear the cobwebs she sensed were beginning to nestle in the dark corners of her mind.

Sharala believed herself to be far too practical a woman to allow foreboding feelings to last long. Less than a minute later, she was confidently making her way down the hallway outside Anit's hospital room toward the nurse's station.

But she had left the lights on in her daughter's room. Whether it was a subconscious decision or not, Sharala would never be able to honestly say, but nevertheless she had left them on.

Sharala preoccupied herself with demanding the head nurse on duty find someone to whom she could lodge a complaint about Dr. Bringleson.

After Anit's body had fallen into a deep and much needed state of sleep, her right eye slowly opened. That eye ... with its diagnosed hypermydrosis, wasn't really experiencing hyper-mydrosis, at all. Its engorged, iridescent blue pupil opened wide and decided it would be more comfortable if the lights were off – and so they turned the lights off.

Then the eye, which had become a window ... in every sense of the word ... and the secret it held, closed once again and slumbered peacefully alongside the mind and body it now shared with Anit Chima.

8

Stones in The Garden

One morning before the sun had yet to make its way above the line of the horizon, a new and mysteriously calming sound permeated Terris' tiny sleeping quarters. He felt it gently vibrating the fine surface hairs of his arms before his brain processed it as sound. It was a low, deep intermittent hum, a steady sound he imagined some great giant would make if he were deep in slumber but suffering mildly from problems with his adenoids. It was as though some great creature was rhythmically exhaling through its nostrils at slow and steady intervals.

He lay in his cot for the better part of an hour, idly imagining what the source of the noise could be. Naturally, his first thoughts were it was some type of chant these strangely patient monks practiced. But this answer didn't sit quite well with him because there were no recognizable words of any language his Western ears could discern. No, what he was feeling deep in his stomach and simultaneously hearing were the vibratory tones of what he could only describe as a "hum." It was his need to urinate more than outright curiosity that motivated him to get up. He lifted his legs over the side of the cot, one at a time, allowing himself to rest momentarily before fetching and using the dark bronze chamber pot tucked just out of sight underneath the bed.

With his bladder empty, he felt lighter and beset with curiosity. He reached for the sturdy wooden stick Erik had hewn for him from a tree he'd found God only knows where a week before. He had been deeply grateful for finally having progressed in his recovery enough to trade his constant Nordic companion for the piece of wood, because walking sticks didn't simply appear in his room at all hours of the day and night and watch him all the damn time. He leaned heavily on the stick, which easily bore the brunt of his weight, which he had lost much of due to being kept primarily on a liquid diet for well over a month. He managed to make his way from his cot to the threshold of the door, but it still took him all of roughly ten painful minutes to make his way out of his quarters and half-way down the wood-slatted corridor, even with the cane.

Li had informed him that he had most likely broken at least two ribs on his left side and they had torn through the soft tissue of his lung. He hadn't really wanted to know much more after that; some things hurt too much to think about. He was still alive and this was really all he needed to know, for now. Stepping gingerly down the narrow corridor in his bare feet, he found the floors to be warm and relaxing.

He had already deduced where he thought the sound might be coming from, and it was a place he had visited several times before with Erik's assistance, so he knew where he was going.

At the end of the corridor to the left, lay a sizable courtyard, the outer edges of which alternated between fauna and meticulously cultivated sand gardens. Each garden had been imprinted with long, calming, equidistant lines indicative of the reflective thoughts pondered by its creator. The greenery in the gardens contained a plethora of what Terris could only assume were herbs utilized for The Keeper's cooking and medicinal purposes. The majority of these plants, leafy greens and multicolored flowers, were wholly unfamiliar to him in appearance. The main area of the courtyard was inlaid with hand hewn, octagonal stone slabs cut straight from the surrounding mountain.

Terris had found the courtyard empty and serene on his past visits, but on this particular morning he was stunned when he saw over one hundred and seventy-five elderly men and women working through the complex movements of some form of Tai Chi. He had neither seen nor heard tales of it in his more than four decades of practicing the martial arts. The low meditative hum he heard was a culmination of this group of people inhaling and exhaling in controlled unison and thus creating a low frequency hum. This was the sound that had pierced his ears, befuddled his mind, and interrupted his sleep? Nearly two hundred bodies, minds and spirits breathing as one at 4:15 in the morning! But where had they all come from?

He had not heard a sound as these ancient bodies made their way step by step over the sharp gravel and rocks lining the courtyard. They were all dressed in khaki or some equally bland color belonging to the earthen-color gradient. Their backs faced him, and they stood equidistant from one another other in five separate rows. Even from this angle, and given the bow of their elderly bodies, their baldheads and white or silver hair respectively, Terris knew none of them could've been younger than seventy. Their feet were bare, with soles that were thick, marred and toughened with age, and by the very rocks upon which they stood. Terris deduced the courtyard had probably been built directly over some long forgotten volcanic vent. Either that, or these octogenarians had developed far more resistance to the foreboding cold than he realized.

At the head of the group stood a Japanese woman who was no taller than a ten-year-old child. Her face was heavily lined and withered with age, yet she stood firm with her back straight. She led the group through the most painfully slow movements Terris had ever seen and he marveled at the amount of breath control and strength these seniors were able to maintain. They fascinated Terris – he had not realized so many elderlies were in the monastery because he had seen no more than a dozen or so of them since his arrival, including the leader of the group, whose name he would later learn was "Yukiro."

He would also discover that she and several others among this group had arrived at "The Keep" - which is what those who lived there called it - when they were still little more than children. Some came as young as thirteen years old. Yukiro, however, had entered the gates when she was seventeen. But their stories were the same. Some unseen voice, an urge, a force felt from within each of them which would not be denied had compelled them all to seek out this unkown, remote place tucked away in the Tian Shan mountains. They were steadfast and firm reminders of how long some of them had waited (as did all within The Keep) for whatever purpose The Creator had for them. The ravages of time had been kinder to them perhaps, but it had not completely spared their mortal flesh from the inevitable, which was betrayed by age and infirmity in the manner of all men.

Terris watched in reverence as these fleshy remnants of a youthful existence toiled gracefully without so much as a whimper of complaint. He would eventually come to learn "The Stones," as they were affectionately called, inhabited the oldest parts and, therefore, the more reclusive areas within the temple. Rarely were more than a dozen of them seen about the whole of the temple during midday hours. And he would become a familiar face among those who had the run and authority of the kitchens.

Terris came from a large family and he learned a long time ago that whoever held the keys to the food coffers held the keys to a man's chance of survival.

So, naturally, once he was able to venture out unaided and alone beyond the corridor outside his sleeping chamber, he went into the passages within the temple that twisted and turned in every direction on the campus until he eventually found his way into the kitchen. The vast kitchen consisted of three interconnected chambers that were divided by partitioned walls fashioned from what Terris guessed were a kind of thin bamboo material similar to rattan. The partitions were arranged in such a way as to create short throughways that ran throughout the entirety of the space. In the center of the kitchen lay an open bed of burning coals that ran the length of the room, upon which sat no less than six giant cauldrons, each filled to the brim with a thick and sumptuous smelling broth.

On any given morning, he would find at least a dozen or so octogenarians stepping lively here and there amongst the steaming pots, stirring, tasting, and dropping in the odd ingredient or a bowl of indiscernible herbs of varying colors.

One was an elderly Caucasian man with the longest mustache Terris had ever seen. He bore a striking resemblance to an actor who played Sherlock Holmes on television in the early '90s. It was one of Terris' favorite television shows, but he was unable to recall the actor's name, although he was fairly certain it was John or Jeremy, or something like that.

The man in the kitchen didn't have a single hair on his head and his face had the appearance of having been pulled very tightly across his bare skull. His head gleamed like a pale billiard ball as he methodically swept the stone floor of the kitchen with an old, modestly bristled, rickety broom. The broom reminded Terris of a well-known picture book his grandmother had once shared with him when he was a child. The book was *Hansel and Gretel*, and the evil witch in the story had a broom that looked very much like the one the man was holding. Terris would often find himself smiling whenever he recalled his first venture into the kitchen at the memory of the elderly men and women who paused in their work just long enough to turn and flash him a welcoming smile. They had not spoken to him then or since; they only smiled and nodded politely before returning to their tasks. At this time, it dawned on him that he had never once seen any of these seniors wearing shoes, sandals or slippers on their feet.

This had been nearly three weeks ago, and the steady low hissing sound had awakened him every morning thereafter at 4:15 a.m. during his recuperation. It was as though, once heard, his body now awaited the sound of it. But this was a new morning, and although it was once again 4:15 a.m. and Terris could again hear the hissing sound, today's noise was different. Today the hissing sounded louder, heavier, and stronger.

And today, Terris was going to make his way to the courtyard without the aid of the walking stick. He rose from his bed and pulled on the modest brown woolen pants and tunic he had been given to wear.

The sheer discipline and resolve of the elderly men and women inspired him. He would rise from his cot each morning he was physically able to and make his way down the narrow wooden corridor unaided, simply to bear witness once again to The Stones in the Garden.

9

The Archangel Michael's Thoughts on Lucifer

I do not know why my brother Lucifer would not heed. I said this to him openly and without malice or pity, "Lucifer, brother, I tell you that God shall have His way in this as in all things that concern Him. The state of Man and His daughter, Earth has vexed Him as of late. Woe to he who has expended the patience of He who loves most. But I tell you on this matter, His mind is set!"

"Are thou also angered with me, Michael?" asked Lucifer.

"Surely, I am not, brother," said the Archangel Michael. "You are the only countenance fit to stand beside our brother, Gabriel. The Creator gave you the rights of Man's heart should any man wish to grant it to you. Even in your disgrace He does not deny you this. Your pride caused you to want for recognition and glory – have you not found this in the hearts and minds of Man? For surely, they know who you are. They bend to your impulsiveness as easy as a sapling sways under the breath of our Father. All that is dark and vile within them, they attribute to you. Do you not see how The Father has purposed you? It is only through you that God may know the truth of a man. Their acceptance or rejection of you. It only saddens me that Mankind seeks comfort in laying the source of their evil ways at your feet, dear brother instead of at their own roots.

"Truly, I say to you that all of Humankind would fall dead were they to behold your glorious features, knowing still the destruction one as beautiful as you can bring," said Michael. "You are clever, my brother, but again, I tell you true that in this matter concerning Humankind, God will have His way."

"I desire only to occupy the Earth along with any who would dwell there with me," replied Lucifer.

"I tell you truly, brother, all know your desire to ravage the Earth. She is beautiful is she not? But this can never be; her pain is too great now. She is weakened and worn as none of us imagined she could ever be," said Michael. "No, no, brother, He loves her far too greatly to burden her further. I tell you right-fully the Earth will not and cannot, for her own sake, be yours."

"But she is beautiful," Lucifer, my brother, replied, as if caught in a dream, which he usually is. A dream of glory beyond that of the Father. A kind of glory God only allows through the filter that is Man. But we, his brothers, already knew the pain that man would bring him. For in the end, it is the nature of all creatures to return to the source of their exis-tence. A day will come when God will choose to reveal Himself, and blinded by His glory and the unfathomable depths of His love, all Mankind will forsake my brother, Lucifer, even so the ground upon which they stand to use their last breath to exhale the names of God.

My brother, crafty and restless as he is, could stand all things except being alone. It brought tears to my eyes to imagine my beautiful brother, second only perhaps to Gabriel, standing on a plateau of the Earth as she with her waters, Mankind and God Himself turned their backs on him. Yes, my brother's purpose often troubled me greatly. Greatly, indeed.

BOOK II

There is a place most human eyes will never see. Nestled high within the snowy mountains of the Asian continent, where sits a temple. There "The Bell of God" is kept in a chamber, sealed before recorded time, when The Creator made His covenant with the treasured Earth before His creation of Man.

In the beginning of the world, only three of Mankind were shown the plan for the coming of the end, and these men recorded what they were told by The Creator, all the while knowing that Man – Humankind, in its arrogance, would bring themselves to disbelieve the prophecies of what was to come. These caretakers, The Keepers of the Bell, were predestined to their task before they were conceived.

Upon reaching the age of independent thought, some as early as twelve or thirteen years of age, would feel the will of The Creator move them to make the journey to this sacred temple. They were compelled to make their way from wherever they were upon the four corners of the Earth to an ancient hidden temple high in the snowy mountains of what is now a province of China. Instinctively, they knew where the sacred place could be found, although the spot had never been marked on any man-made map.

Once there, they were welcomed unquestioningly, judged neither by age or skin, nor the place of origin.

Each was welcomed warmly at the door, as though expected – which, unbeknownst to them, they were. And each finding within the temple walls the answers to questions regarding their purpose on the Earth. Men and women of different creeds, colors and cultures would remain waiting, some even up unto the end of their mortal days. Here they waited and trained their body and mind for what was yet to come – the signal, the ringing of a bell crafted by God and mounted by His holy angels, before being sealed in a sacred chamber away from the eyes of man. A chamber that had for centuries remained ominous and silent...until tonight.

10

The Keep

1:53 a.m.–One Thousand One-Hundred and Eighty-Five Days before Maia Joy Knightly disappeared.

Yum turned over on his back and sighed heavily and resolutely in the darkness. He knew what time it was – it was always the same time – 1:53 a.m. He also knew he would awaken and turn at this time, this same time, no matter where on Earth his body might happen to lay.

I am an old man, he thought. *The old do not often sleep as well or as soundly as the young.* Yum thought these things all the while knowing they were no more connected one to the other than he was to the rest of humanity.

There was a familiar chill in his room, and by the glow of the moonlight filtering through the few remaining wooden slats of his window he imagined he could see his breath as he exhaled heavily for the second time. He shifted his position on the simple cushioned pallet that served as his bed and waited for the weariness from his daily labor to once again overtake his elderly frame. He was having The Dream again. The dream in which he heard the low baritone reverberations of a temple gong being struck repeatedly in a slow methodic rhythm somewhere far beyond the valleys of the Celestial Mountains in which he lived.

It was a deep, resonating sound that once heard, moved through his body with ease and purpose. Yum dreaded the dream and yet was soothed by its consistency. It never changed – at some point during his nightly repose he would simply become aware that he was "awake" in the dream. He would hear the deep resonating gong and at times feel the sound as its tone reverberated through his elderly sinews. Eventually the sound he had come to dread, but also found a deep sense of comfort in, would lull him back into a deep sleep...and then it would be dawn. But in those moments of subconscious reality, he could feel each heavy baritone tone of the gong reverberating through his body. Yes, he literally "felt" the sound.

He turned over on his back and exhaled wearily in the darkness. His eyes were open, but he knew he was not awake. This was The Dream that had haunted him for the better part of his fifty-two years, a dream that Yum found maddening in its sheer simplicity. From the time he was a ten- year-old boy growing up in the East End District of London, he would awaken in the dream, in a small but comfortable bed in a darkened room. He could always sense the room was indeed his, but its location and his connection to it, he simply could not fathom.

And then there was The Sound, a slow, rhythmic, deeply resonate and repetitive tone he could only liken to the ritual gonging of singing bowls found in the temples of the Buddha. It was a hauntingly beautiful sound and upon hearing it, Yum had the sense of a life purpose or task having been fulfilled.

On more than one occasion during this waking dream, Yum had shed tears of joy at the sound of the bell. But he soon learned his dream self was unable to ascertain the exact location or direction of the bell. He would often find himself cognizant enough to attempt to count the methodic bellows of the gong resounding in his mind, only to drift back into regular sleep time and awaken in his own bed. For many years of his youth, Yum would unsuccessfully attempt to recapture the rapture he felt in his dream. Or try to understand why the vision of it always ended at 1:53 a.m.

Without fail, over the course of fifty-two years, upon waking from the dream, Yum would find it was exactly 1:53 a.m. Always. But now, tonight, as he lay in the dream listening to the sound of a bell he could not find, he reminded himself that he was now a man of sixty-two. Perhaps not old to some, but most certainly beyond the prime of life for many. He was an old man now, and the intermittent sleep of the elderly was not the sweet slumber of the young.

The dream that plagued him for these many years was not unlike the occasional bouts of pain or gas that beleaguers the aged.

Yum inhaled deeply and exhaled patiently before reaching down to scratch his left foot. He was mildly annoyed that the deep reverberating tones of the gong in his dream had caused the flesh on the top of his foot to vibrate and itch. The elderly man's eyes opened wide and the breath hitched in his chest as he slowly removed his fingers from his foot and ran his hand up the length of his leg, thigh and upper torso until it came to rest on his bony chest. Yum's heart was now pounding hard enough to burst through the flesh and bone holding it in place, and into the trembling sweaty palm covering it.

He sat upright in his narrow cot and remained absolutely motionless as the melodious tone of something yet unseen reverberated though the darkness before settling upon his skin. He could actually sense the tangible vibration of the air around him as the wave of sound passed over and through his elderly being. The quivering of the hairs on his head and the nape of his neck caused him to shudder. He could hear the sound of both bare and many sandaled feet moving about in the hallway that lay beyond his chamber. There was confusion and a budding panic in the excited but muffled voices of the Keepers of the Temple, when a quick and somewhat alarming, albeit respectful rapping sounded at his door.

"Yes. Come in," Yum spoke calmly as he rose from his bed, his hands already seeking out his kimono.

"Master Yum," said the young man at his door, whose name was "Milos." His question was cut short as the resonant all-encompassing tone of the gong sounded again.

Seconds later, the walls of Yum's chamber (and he guessed the very walls of the temple) shuddered violently from its core of stone and wood foundation. The young man at the door stared at Yum, wide-eyed and ashen-faced before a one-sided, bashful smile crossed his face. Yum realized he and the young man shared the same impression of that last shudder. "Ecstasy" – that is how the entire temple shook ... as if in expectant ecstasy of an impending birth. The elder man swiftly secured his kimono around his frail frame with a brusque tug of a sash.

"Come, let us see what is happening this night," Yum's face shone like a beacon, and he placed a reassuring hand on Milo's forearm as he made his way past the younger man and into the corridor outside his sleep chamber. Milos dutifully closed the door of the elder man's quarters before following closely behind him.

On either side of the corridor, Yum met the gaze of each of the thirty or so resident Keepers of Temple Khan Tengri. They had all stepped forth from their quarters after hearing the mysterious gong and were doing their best to contain their mounting concerns.

The Keepers, like himself, had been handpicked by The Creator to be in this place at this time. But it was the commanding voice of the newest resident that made Yum pause in his stride momentarily.

"What the hell is that?" Terris' deep baritone American voice caught Yum off guard, while it simultaneously demanded an answer from no one in particular but an answer nonetheless.

A glint of metal suddenly caught the attention of Yum's eye, and off to his left, he saw Paolo. He was just able to catch a glimpse of the crucifix in the cradle of Paolo's neck, which he had been fingering between the thick pads of his thumb and forefinger, before he hastily returned it to its resting place within the folds of his wool tunic. Yum saw fear in Paolo's eyes and a prayer moving upon his lips.

"I will tell you as soon as I know," Yum assured them, before turning again to Milos. "Where is Shihan?"

"Come," was all the anxious young man would reply before ushering Yum away from the other men. Yum and Milos made their way through the dim, torch-lit corridors of the temple.

The older man followed behind Milos, and in the midst of all that was happening he lamented his age and allowed himself the briefest moment of envy as he admired the younger man's full head of hair. It was black and shiny as onyx, with the exception of two wide swaths of steel grey strands that stretched back from his temples right to the tip of the thick, braided ponytail looped around his neck before falling midway down his back between his broad shoulders.

Yum calculated that if Milos ever chose to let his mane of hair fall free from the braided and looped ponytail, it would surely fall well past the woven leather belt he wore about his waist. He tried to recall how long Milos had been at the temple. Surely the Greek was well into his fifties by now, but Yum could only see the sun-drenched, solemn fourteen-year-old who had arrived at the temple one spring afternoon carrying nothing except the rolled blanket strapped to his back. Had it truly been forty years? Yum shook his head as if to bring himself back into present time and the task at hand. At times, it was difficult not to think about how this place had taken the best years of life away from so many. *And for what purpose,* he wondered.

The two men descended a short flight of stone stairs at the base of which stood two wooden doors.

The incessant gong sounded again and the doors shuddered from the vibration. Milos only hesitated a moment, taking an audible breath before reaching out his hand and opening the doors. He then stepped aside to allow Yum to pass through the entrance before him. Yum entered the dimly lit corridor with a visibly shaken Milos following closely behind.

"I will go alone," said Yum, as he held up a hand without turning to look at his companion. "You may return to the others if you wish."

"Yes, Master Yum," Milo made no attempt to mask his relief. Yum gathered up the folds of his Kimono and made his way down the corridor.

The gong sound was coming every minute or so – slow, methodical, and soothing. It penetrated throughout the temple and the very fiber of his being. The deep reverberating tones echoed through the air until the strike of the next tone, a sound that was powerful enough to cause even the dust under Yum's feet to rise from the floor. Just a few steps from where he stood there was another set of stairs. They were carved from stone and led into a narrow, damp hallway that had also been hewn into the very stone of the mountain by hands far more ancient than those now present. The end of the hallway opened into a cavernous chamber, at the end of which stood two massive wood doors well in excess of forty feet in height.

The doors were deeply set into a rough wall of solid rock and were flanked on either side by torches that burned with a preternatural blue flame. The torchlight revealed the doors had been constructed from the intact trunks of what man now recognizes as prehistoric Redwood trees found in the Americas.

Each door consisted of four tree trunks lined side by side and sanded to a smooth finish before being adorned with ancient symbols, the meaning of which had long since been forgotten by mortal men – if they had ever been known to them. An impossibly thick rope that could only have been constructed by the hands of some unknown giant was mounted across the entire width of both doors, secured at the center seam by a twelve-foot tall ancient seal made of clay.

The circumference and width of this seal was no less than that of three broad-shouldered men standing side by side. The seal was also elaborately and quite deeply etched in the ancient writing adorning the wood of the great doors. The incessant rhythmic sound of the unseen gong beyond the doors sounded once again, and the doors heaved outward slightly, like a heavily pregnant woman in the beginning throws of labor. Directly in front of the doors, with his back to Yum, stood Shihan, the first Keeper.

It had been rumored that Shihan was at least one hundred and four years old, but his back was still straight and his gait steady. His hands were still strong enough to split fully grown bamboo tree trunks using only his thumb and forefinger. Anyone who spoke with him for more than an hour couldn't possibly believe him to be any less than a hundred and four, anymore than they could believe the doors he now stood before had not been sealed by God.

Although Yum couldn't say for certain whether or not God had indeed placed the seal upon those massive doors, he could certainly attest to the fact that someone or something much greater than himself or anything he could name upon this earth was ringing what sounded like an enormous gong inside of a chamber on the other side of them. A chamber that had been secured with a holy seal some countless number of years ago ... a seal that remained as of yet, unbroken.

Yum hadn't realized he was shaking as he approached Shihan with habitual reverence and stood silently at the elder's left shoulder. He gave his usual methodic bow of respect even though his master did not acknowledge his presence. Shihan knew that in Yum's heart, his reservation and reverence were duly placed in the direction of the events at hand, even if Yum himself was unaware of it. Both men then stood in silence before the immense wooden doors and the gigantic ancient seal and waited for the next toll of the unseen gong.

Tian Shan Mountains are north and west of the Xinjiang Province of China. These Celestial Mountains are nestled in a hidden valley, and near its peak is Temple Khan Tengri, the sacred place of that which man calls God. The God of the Christians, the Jews, the Muslims, the Hindus and the Buddhists – The One God, The Creator and That Which Forms. And unlike many of the places and things in China and around the world, there were no stories or legends to be heard (or told of) about this most sacred and secret of places.

But there were always the occasional rumors. It is difficult for a tale to be told or fabricated about a place that no one but the Almighty knows even exists. A place built by the servants of God to and for His purpose. Temple Khan Tengri had stood long before man had tongue to give it a name. It was a place built by celestial hands for a celestial purpose. A place occupied from the dawn of Mankind by those souls handpicked by God. There was no map, guide or marker for the temple. It was a place put into man's mind by The Creator. Put into his mind like a compass so it could not be ignored or pushed aside for lesser aims. The temple was occupied by those compelled to find their way to its threshold, or die trying. One could contemplate how many souls had been driven mad in their desire, their need to make the journey, but had no ability to reach the temple gates.

The gates were not hidden from those who were meant to find them and who were meant to pass through them. Somewhere among the icy peaks of the Tian Shan, a man or woman weighted with a purpose from God will find the gates. A solitary black gate of iron stands where nothing should stand, a gate that opens onto the path of Eternal Spring. Here, there is a Winter garden where a single cherry blossom tree grows, a giant tree that is pleasing to the eye of God, and whose trunk stands firm to mark the passage of time. A man looks from the trunk of this grand blossom and sets his eye to fall upon the sacred Temple of The Heavenly Gate of Temple Khan Tengri.

Now, and as it has been from the beginning of time, a Keeper greets him at the end of the path and welcomes him with an expected nature and outstretched arms, for all who arrive have come at the behest of The Almighty. And on this night, deep within the bowels of the temple, Master Shihan and Yum stood trapped in time before the immense doors, its seal, and the wall of sound emanating from within the chamber.

The elder master's countenance was unreadable as he stood calmly with his arms tucked within the front folds of his evening kimono.

"Yum, it would seem your dream has at last manifest." Relieved, Shihan spoke quietly.

"Master, I assure you that I never dreamed this. I have never known the source of the sounds in my dream. Yet, it is unmistakably the sound I heard. The sound of a distant temple bell."

"Yum, do you know the meaning of your name?"

"It is he who listens for the cries of the world," said Yum.

"In the Korean language, yes – but in Japanese, your name means "The Dream" – the Dream who listens for the cries of the world."

The two of them stood silently side-by-side in this manner for a long moment, until at last Yum's voice somehow cut quietly through the unearthly toll of the gong.

"And is the world crying?"

"This I cannot answer, Master Yum."

Yum let another long moment pass as the wall of sound continued to pass over and through them.

"But...? he pressed, having become familiar with the master's response patterns over the years.

"But... if I had to guess, I would guess there is a rather large temple bell within the chamber," said Shihan, in an unnervingly calm voice.

"And someone is ringing it?" The thought of trying to calculate the sheer size of the hands managing to ring such a gong made the hairs on Yum's arms stand on end.

"There is but One." His master spoke with the same unperturbed demeanor and without averting his gaze from the doors.

"What shall we do, Shihan?"

At this, Shihan did look away and then directly at Yum.

"We shall do what we have always done – wait with patience and preparedness."

"Should we not breech the seal?" said Yum.

"The seal was placed there by God, and when the time comes for it to be broken and the doors opened, I trust He will do just that, but in His own time."

As if on cue, the next sounding of the gong cracked the ancient seal holding the doors in place. A large angry fissure coursed through the thick clay disc with a sound like the cracking of the earth itself.

Except to turn his head calmly toward the thunderous sound of the cracking disc, Shihan stood motionless. Conversely, a deeply startled Yum gave into his human nature and retreated a step. The cracking seal continued to sound as though the mountain on which they stood had suddenly been wrenched in two, as if it were a piece of thick fabric being rendered apart by unseen, perhaps even ungodly hands. The sound momentarily drowned out the tonal bellows of the gong that lay within the chamber.

With the next sounding of the bell, the doors thrust forward un-tethered, causing great chunks of the broken seal to fall away amid a blinding plume of dust as the bulging doors finally disturbed the centuries of old dirt and dust that had collected at its base.

"Master Yum, please gather the Keepers in the courtyard," said Shihan, making the request sound as if he were merely asking Yum to gather the others for the evening meal. His eyes wide, Yum began to back away swiftly, hesitating only when he saw the elder man had once again turned his full attention back to the closed doors.

"Master, will you not come with me?"

"No, I shall wait here a few moments longer. I should like to greet The Almighty as I have greeted all of those who have entered the temple. For He is our most honored guest, is He not?"

Yum bowed respectfully and hurried back through the dark corridor toward Milos and the other Keepers.

Shihan immediately regretted having dismissed Yum so soon. For at this moment, the centurion's chest was full of wonder at the awesome force that had caused the seal, which was at least six feet thick, to fissure. His spirit swelled at the complexity of all he was witnessing, and he wondered if Yum had yet realized how The Creator had used him. Surely Yum recognized the manifestation of the dream that had plagued his mind for so long. And surely, he knew the meaning of his name "Yum," which is "dream" in Japanese and "he who listens to the cries of the world."

Was the world not crying this night? Was the bell not at this very moment tolling at the hand of the unknown, the unseen will of God? How calm Yum had remained this night. As well he should have, as it would seem his entire life had been groomed to prepare him for this moment, which should, by all rights, fill the stoutest of men with fear. But, Master Yum, having been ordained for this task from birth or perhaps before, was already prepared to bear whatever weight or burden this night would bring. His countenance of strength and unmanu-factured calm would serve the other Keepers well when he – Shihan – was gone.

Yes, all was in order, just as it had always been at Temple Khan Tengri, where The Keepers of God waited with patience and preparedness. Shihan greatly envied Yum, and he smiled with the joy of "knowing."

The next toll of the gong came with such vibratory force that the double doors made of dateless trees, which long ago had become hard as granite, flexed outward like a great muscle, splitting the ancient sacred seal completely in half, causing it to crash to the floor. Though the doors had not parted at their seam, the sheer power of the sound of the cracking seal fell so heavily against Shihan's chest, he was forced to retreat a few steps to steady himself.

Even at one hundred and eighteen years of age, which was indeed his true age, the old master remained far from frail. He had the mind, body and spirit of a well-built, healthy man in his early forties, and he was not one who was easily moved after having made the decision to stand his ground. However, in the midst of his retreat from the falling seal, the Geta he had been wearing upon his feet had been inadvertently removed and neatly placed to one side just to the right of were he now stood. Shihan stared at his shoes in wonderment and understanding.

The sound of the ancient seal crashing to the ground brought Keepers of all ages running into the inner chamber to Shihan's side, in fear for his life. They had already gathered together and been waiting anxiously in the outer chamber of the temple.

"STOP AND REMOVE YOUR SHOES!" The sheer volume of Shihan's voice was enough to stop every man and woman in mid-stride. There was not one among them who had ever heard the elder man raise his voice in such a manner in all their days combined at the temple. Those who were wearing sandals, woven slippers, socks, or Japanese footwear known as "Geta" on their feet, removed them and piled them up just outside the door. The gong remained eerily quiet while they did so, and it kept silent as many of them crowded their way into the room and looked up at the massive doors.

When the next bellowing of the still unseen gong came, it caused a catastrophic fissure to rip through the surface of the solid stonewall both above and below the weighty doors. As though the very mountain was on the verge of being split in half, and then – as if of one mind or one unimaginable force – the mammoth doors were flung apart. Most people were knocked to the ground, and many of the Keepers screamed in terror and fled from the room. Shihan kept his footing, shielding his face with both arms from the heavy chunks of stone and razor-sharp shards of granite that flew across the room as the heavy doors, still fully intact, hit the solid rock walls to which they had been soldered for more millennia than Humankind could remember.

A blinding cloud of dust blew forth from the chamber on a wave of virginal air so fresh, so sweet smelling and clean, that it burned the polluted lungs of the men who inhaled it. Those who had already been knocked down got on their knees and found themselves moved to tears as something deep within them realized that surely this must be the air of Heaven, or perhaps the very breath of God. Shihan lowered his arms from his face and peered beyond the settling dust into the open chamber, which by now had gone deathly silent. Everything became still, even the dust hung in the air as if transfixed in time. In the space just beyond the threshold of the chamber lay a seemingly infinite darkness.

Shihan thought perhaps he was looking into a doorway that opened into the farthest reaches of space. His humanity caused his breath to hitch in his chest. Somewhere within him he found that he had hoped the heavenly realms of the afterlife would not be so bleak. Then, as if in answer to his fears, the inner chamber became illuminated with a soft, golden light for which there could be no earthly source. Shihan heard at least two more Keepers behind him cry out in fear, before they also ran back into the open area of the temple, and perhaps beyond. But he did not dare avert his eyes to confirm their departure. Slowly, the glow within the chamber began to grow and pulsate like a living heart. The soft, steady, golden glow soon revealed a massive chamber with a ceiling that reached at least thirty feet high.

The walls themselves were impossibly smooth and the color of a clear night sky, an intensely deep dark blue, almost imperceptivity inlaid with iridescent gold and flecks of white light that moved upon its surface like living, sentient things. It was like looking out onto the many galaxies of an unknown space. In fact, it was space. At some point in time and space, which the current observers knew nothing about, space had been brought to this place and into the very chamber that now stood open before them. Even within this place there was something else, a place of light, a place of peace, something in the vastness that was, even now, reaching out to them and embracing them with love, hope and happiness.

"It is not possible," said Milos, who had quietly sidled up next to Shihan and now whispered with tears streaming down his face. Shihan smiled at the sound of wonderment in the younger man's voice. Again, as if in response, the unseen temple bell tolled from somewhere deep within the cavernous chamber.

Every man, including Shihan, was forced to cover their ears as the gold translucent light within the chamber was joined by a similar pulsating orb which was blue in color and which had also come from somewhere deep within the depths of the chamber. The sound of the immense bell rang eleven more consecutive times, and preceding each toll there was the manifestation of a blue, glowing translucent orb, until they totaled thirteen chimes in all.

The orbs then elongated into individual pillars of light, floating approximately three feet above the floor of the chamber, each expanding until they measured anywhere from six to nine feet in height. Seven of the pillars changed from their original deep blue hue to the distinct colors of fiery orange, a dark green, gold, purple, teal, silver, and copper. The remaining six were variations of their solid-colored companions with the colors black, red and white being noticeably absent.

In all, thirteen pillars had manifested themselves and when the bell tolled thirteen times, it again fell silent. Silent as a tomb, it was as if time itself had suddenly held its breath. There was no sound or movement in the room, aside from the pillars of light, which continued to pulsate in sync with one another as though they shared the same beating heart. One of the younger Keepers let escape a stifled and most likely unintended and pitiful sob from his lips.

The sound seemed to prompt the pillars to tentatively float forth closer to the threshold of the chamber. They passed ethereally over the entryway of the sacred room and through the thick veil of dust still hanging motionless in the air. As they entered the anteroom where Shihan and the other Keepers stood transfixed, the air became charged with a palatable and peaceful energy.

Several of the Keepers, who had just gotten back to their feet, fell once again to their knees in supplication, as the living lights positioned themselves in an inverted semi-circle on the chamber's threshold from which they had emerged. Shihan could now clearly hear at least three of the Keepers fervently muttering prayers in their respective native tongues, with a German Keeper by the name of Gunaar being the most distinct among them. The luminous columns remained still for a long moment, and Shihan sensed the divine lights were somehow "taking in" the situation. The pillars were observing them, even though they possessed no human qualities or features of note. Shihan's senses told him this much was true: the situation was as new and strange for these unearthly beings as it was for the human beings.

A low, almost imperceptible hum began to permeate the room, and Shihan thought perhaps the entire mountain must be humming. He perceived movement in his peripheral vision and turned his gaze to find the most recent arrival to the temple standing by his right shoulder. It was Terris Jackson. The American had already taken another tentative step toward the entities, and his dark skin glowed in their amber light. Terris' clean-shaven head was cocked slightly to one side as if he were intently listening to something. The center pillar, which was the tallest of them, floated forward in response to Terris' approach.

The pillar was a deep and fiery golden color, and it appeared to serve as the dividing point for the remaining twelve pillars.

In that moment, every human in the room stood motionless, not daring to breathe or blink.

"Do you hear it?" Terris' resonant voice queried no one in particular.

"Yeah, mate … I hear it," replied Randle, a ruddy-faced Keeper with a thick Australian accent in his mid-twenties. He was still on his knees as if in prayer, and he had spoken without taking his eyes off the glowing lights.

"Watashi, mo," the Moshi twins chimed in simultaneously. They were standing directly to the left of Shihan, side by side as always. The twins hailed from an unknown province in Japan and were perhaps the most mysterious of all the temple's inhabitants. They were both exactly five feet six and half inches tall, a svelte and stately fraternal pair. One male and one female, their skin was translucent and smooth with sharply angled facial features. The identical outward physical attributes of the pair were asexual in appearance, and once fully clothed in their loose-fitting robes, any differences between them were virtually imperceptible. Their eyes were an unusually light tawny brown, set widely apart, and they could easily be described as appearing otherworldly. There were many in the temple who regularly avoided contact with the twins, and more than one report had reached Shihan's ears about one or both siblings' eyes having inexplicably changed color.

The two had arrived at the gates of The Keep ten years before, walking hand in hand through waist deep snow at night during a lunar eclipse, when they were just thirteen years old. From that night on, one would never be seen more than five yards away from the other, and they would only answer to the single name of "Moshi." Shihan had given Li the curious, if not daunting task of counting each of the twin's eyelashes, only to discover that not only did they have the same number of eyelashes, but they also shared the same growth pattern.

Shihan had long suspected they were most likely symbiotic, as well, because they rarely spoke to anyone unless spoken to first. Over the years, the old man had come to believe just about every strange rumor he had ever heard about the Moshi twins.

Gunaar, the German Keeper who had immediately taken to prayer upon seeing the pillars emerge from the chamber, slowly rose from his crouched position like a marionette whose strings were far too loose.

"Ja, ich hore es auch," his tongue was foreign to most in the room, but the reverence shining on his face and resounding in his voice was unmistakable. Shihan looked at him knowingly, for he suddenly understood what was happening. He knew this man could not speak Japanese, yet he himself heard the words "And let us form Man in Our likeness" – as it was repeated over and over in his own lost and presumably long forgotten native dialect of Ainu.

"What do you hear?" Shihan inquired of Gunaar, speaking to the man in perfect German.

"Und lassen Sie uns ein Mann in Unserem Gleichnis," a clearly shaken Gunaar replied in a hushed whisper and without taking his wide eyes from the pillars of light. Seconds later, in unison, both Randle and Terris recited the phrase in English. "And let us form Man in our likeness."

"And you, Yum?" Shihan's gaze returned to the pulsating lights as he awaited a reply. "What do you hear?"

"I … I hear nothing, Shihan. I hear nothing," Yum replied with reverence. He was still staring at the pillars, but his voice was tinged with an air of failure, as though he had been found unworthy.

"I speak a fair bit of German, Master, but he can't possibly speak Xhosa. I barely remember it from school." This statement came from the voice of the tallest and most imposing of The Keepers, a formidable and dark-skinned African man by the name of Shylo, who stood an impressive seven foot, six inches tall. "It … they are speaking Xhosa, plain as anything," he added.

"A South African dialect, I believe," Shihan spoke calmly and with understanding.

"Yes. South Africa," Shylo conceded, before taking a step forward in his newfound understanding. Within minutes, five more Keepers had stepped forward having heard what the others could not. This included the Keepers Milos, Paolo, Erik, Yukiro and another female whose name was Elisheva. All of them approached the semicircle of the illuminated entities as though each had been called by name.

Shihan's attention was momentarily taken away from those he had observed over the years, some since they were but children, as they stood before the luminous pillars. And his eyes, not yet faded by any maladies, were drawn toward the void's darkness beyond the doorway from which those entities, if this was indeed what they were to be called, had emerged. There within the chamber lay a void that was nearly tangible, and he thought he saw but had most assuredly sensed one large mass moving within and yet another moving deeper within that. The mere idea of what or rather who was moving just beyond his feeble human perception stirred his heart and had apparently also heard his thoughts.

A voice came to Shihan inside his head – a voice he had heard several times throughout his time in the temple. It was akin to the sound of the wind blowing across the peaks and within the valleys of the Celestial Mountains. It was, however, the first time Shihan could make out the words the mighty voice was speaking. Tears of gratitude coursed down his cheeks and joy filled his fluttering heart. All at once, his body was enveloped in a kind of warmth he would never be fully capable of describing with mere words. He knew what he was feeling was the divine embrace of The Most Holy One.

"Yuichi," the voice called to him by the name given to him at birth. "I am solaced by you. I am much pleased with you, but remove your gaze from My form lest your sight be blighted, My most humble one."

The voice was kind, like a warm liquid surrounding and flowing through all his senses, and he shuddered violently, knowing his body was rejoicing! With tears streaming down his face, Shihan obediently curbed his natural human curiosity and averted his eyes from the living void in the doorway. This man, on this mountain, in the presence of that which he perceived as his creator, turned aside as was commanded. Without a question in his heart, he had achieved that which the prototype of his kind had not. He truly was Yuichi – an adored son – as he had been when his mother had first given him this name.

God had just spoken his name, and it was the voice of the Divine that would reverberate in his ears until the day came when he would join Him in another realm. The old Keeper fell upon his knees in complete reverence.

Yum rushed to his master's aid, thinking perhaps the present events had proved too overwhelming for the aging man to bear. Unbeknownst to all save Shihan, The Creator again spoke to his mind.

"Faithful one, I bestow upon you The Iyrin ... the gift of seeing your life's purpose fulfilled."

In the next moment, it was as though God Himself had inhaled, holding all available air within His holy countenance. The thirteen pillars of light suddenly became very much alive as they each turned a deep shade of amber. And in unison, eleven of the pillars floated forward and enveloped the eight men and three women, who were standing foremost on their feet in awe before them. One pillar for each of them, Yum and Shihan witnessed with their own mouths agape as the essence of the Divine entered the bodies of the chosen eleven. As the lights touched them, each Keeper inhaled deeply as if breathing in the sweet fragrance of Heaven itself. They inhaled but did not exhale, as their chests were now abnormally swollen and full of a life force no longer solely their own.

And there they remained with their breath held and their eyes opened wide in reverence while accepting the Divine as if this was the long-awaited arrival of a loved one finally come home.

Just as they themselves had each been accepted into The Keep – so now did they accept this awesome gift from The Creator. All continued to watch in wide-eyed wonder as their brothers and sisters alike were lifted eight feet off the ground. Each was suspended and enveloped in an amber light with their bodies contorting with their arms flung out from their sides and their backs arched to what seemed to be the very limits of their human physiology.

Their eyes remained opened wide with an unspeakable expression of wonder and awe, and Shihan knew that in some way they were being made privy to the secrets of the universe. He experienced a flicker of envy, which was soon overshadowed by the pride and privilege of being chosen to bear witness to the events unfolding before him. The men and women remained suspended in the air like ragdolls that had been lifted by their midsections by an unseen hand.

Their heads lolled to one side, yet their eyes remained transfixed toward the inner chamber from which the pillars had emerged. One of the other Keepers still present, a young man named Lucius, suddenly screamed in terror as the ground began to vibrate. It did not shake as if by an earthquake; instead, it shook as if the Earth's life force was working its way upward toward the temple, from somewhere deep within the planet's core.

The remaining Keepers, including Yum, covered their ears as the vibration of the Earth worked its way from underneath their feet and into the air surrounding them.

Shihan felt as if his head would vibrate right off the top of his spine, and he could feel his innards moving in a most unnatural and uncomfortable manner.

Some of the remaining men and women were crying out in terror, and Shihan would soon understand why. He and the others in the room had thus far witnessed the unfathomable, the melding of the Divine's spirit with the unclean flesh of man.

At the moment of the completion, the chosen men and women shuddered and their meager garments fell away from their bodies. They floated in the air, heads and eyes lolling before each other as naked sons and daughters of man. And before anyone present had ample time to comprehend exactly what was happening, there came forth guttural cries of pain from each of them.

Shihan and the rest watched in terror as the flesh of the earth, which now housed the spirit of the Divine, completely flushed itself of all human disease, foreign matter, poison, and all manner of impurities. Those who had been chosen now writhed about in pain and unbridled agony as fluid and masses of varying consistencies, mucus and excrement freely drained from every open orifice of their bodies and onto the stone floor. Shihan witnessed the expulsion of several fleshy black tumors from Erik, and there was no mistaking that the quiet scholar had, at one time, been a very heavy smoker.

All they had ever taken into the temples of the flesh for which they were responsible, now lay in a foul-smelling mass of steaming viscous mucus, fluid, and feces upon the floor. At the cessation of this purge, each of them was returned to the Earth, naked and unconscious, as gently as if a mother's hand was settling her children in for a sound evening's sleep. Only these children had been laid squarely beside the impurities their bodies had just expelled.

Shihan felt a wave of disgust pass over him as he looked at the men and women upon the floor. He felt shame run over him in such a way as to cause his knees to buckle. He realized this is what the sons of men had become, and to see them naked and lying in their own excrement and disease brought tears to the old master's eyes. He realized that for all he had done to try and live a pure and worthy life – and to guide others to do the same – in the end, this is ultimately what man had become. This is what man was! How dare any such creature think himself worthy of the attentions of God?

Shihan's breath hitched in his chest and he began to sob like a small child at the pitiful sight before him. These men and women lay upon the ground in vile expelled matter that stood as a visceral reminder of man's humanity and his natural lack of humility. Did not even the humblest of men take pride in that? The stench before him was foul beyond description.

And just when the old man thought he could take no more, there again came a loud, cracking noise. Before it had come from somewhere far above the mountain and echoed across the night sky like a sonic boom. But in this very second, the sound could in no way be mistaken for anything ever conceived by mortal man or human thought. It also did not generate from above or outside the room in which they now stood.

The sound, a deafening, bone-shattering combination of a crack and a boom had been generated from the air in the room where they stood. It sounded as if the very fabric of time and space had been ripped apart by some great hand. Those who had somehow managed to remain during this most unusual event were blown backwards and laid out flat on their backs as though hit point blank in the chest by some unseen cannonball. Even Shihan was unable to endure the force of the shockwave the sound brought forth. He, too, found himself splayed out upon his back on the floor. And then, just as quickly and mysteriously, all became unnaturally still, as if time itself had been sucked out of the room.

A deep and palpable silence settled upon the place, and no living thing dared move or speak for a long time. When Shihan ventured to tentatively raise his head, he saw a preternatural amber glow emanating from the bodies of the men and women still lying unconscious and naked on the floor. It was especially bright in Terris. His skin looked as if he had been infused with liquid gold.

The old man's eyes filled with tears of joy and concern for them. The glow dissipated into the air above them like a fine mist and was gone.

In that instant, Shihan no longer saw eleven unconscious human beings, but the essence of the Divine – lying in the filth of humanity.

Shihan swiftly got to his feet and removed his kimono jacket, revealing the muscular torso and arms of a man in his late thirties in the sleeveless tunic he wore underneath. He carefully approached Terris, the newest of them, and was instantly comforted and proud of the faith of such a man to step forth as he did, only to suffer in that faith. He disregarded the foulness in which the unconscious man lay and wrapped him up in his robe, lifting him effortlessly and gently cradling him in his arms as if he were a small, shivering child. Sensing perhaps the worst might be over, three older Keepers then tentatively entered the room and made their way over to the Moshi twins, who lay curled together in a fetal position.

"Master," one of them stammered almost painfully in Shihan's direction. "Master, they are dead!"

"No! Take your robes and cover them. Bathe them and get them into warm beds," said Shihan, his voice sure and confident.

"They are not to be left alone, not even for a moment. Go! Do as I say! Go! Go!" Shihan's voice was direct, but he was nearly pleading for them to move swiftly.

The elderly trio moved quickly, expertly swaddling and carrying the twins away as though they weighed no more than two infant birds.

Yum and Li attended to those who still lay unconscious and followed their master's lead by having Keepers supply blankets or remove their robes. They would then cover and carefully lift each of the unconscious chosen ones from the stone floor, before carrying their charges gently and quietly in the direction of the bathhouses and sleeping chambers. Yum sent word to the kitchens to fill every cauldron with water and bring it to a boil.

"Take them and wash them well with hot water. Then, put them in fresh beds," Li continually repeated the instructions.

The Keepers murmured with reverence amongst themselves about the recent events, as they gathered fresh linens and clean garments from various cubbies, storage rooms and pantries throughout the temple.

When Shihan returned to the chamber room after having delivered Terris to the bathhouse to be cleaned and dressed, both Li and Yum looked to him for further direction with more than a cautionary glance at the dark space that lay beyond the still open inner chamber doors. Neither dared mention there were still two pillars of light that had emerged from the supernatural void, and which were yet to be accounted for.

Had they slipped somewhere back within the shadows of that darkened chamber? Li, for one, couldn't help but feel they were being observed, and the thought caused him to shiver slightly.

"Shall we have fresh broth prepared?" Yum asked nervously, to bring their attention back to the immediate task at hand. He had noticed the chill that ran through Li's body and thought perhaps they could all use a good, hot cup of broth to help their minds begin processing everything they had just witnessed.

"Yes, yes, of course," replied Shihan, who very seriously doubted anyone, especially those who were still unconscious, would be eating anything anytime soon. Shihan supervised things until the last of the Keepers had left the room and, at last, he was alone. He then quickly walked to the far corner of the alcove and picked up a freestanding iron candleholder holding a single wax candle. Using the flame from one of the wall torches, he lit the solitary stem of wax. He quietly and calmly approached the black empty space that existed between the mangled stone doors that had kept the space sacred and secure for so many years.

Carefully, he placed the candle so it stood in the center of the threshold. There, in the far right corner of the room, were two faint pulsating blue pillars of light, lined side by side. They were so faint that he had to squint his eyes to be certain he saw them. But they were there, and he had the distinct feeling they were ... at rest.

For the second time that evening, Shihan was moved to tears. He muttered the word "Arigato" and bowed deeply before taking the candle and quietly retreating away from the threshold. But he remained in the outer chamber, as there was one more thing the old master felt compelled to do. Three industrious Keepers returned to the entrance of the room with steaming buckets of hot water and rags with which to clean, just as he was making his way toward the door. He stared blankly at them for a moment, somewhat surprised at the timing of their arrival. He said nothing until Kameron, an even-tempered, ex-military man from Belgium and the eldest of the three, dared speak.

"Master ... come away. We will clean and scrub the floor. We will remove the stench of it." Kameron spoke firmly and with purpose.

Shihan motioned for them to proceed, and there was only the briefest of hesitation on their part as Shihan himself reached for one of the buckets and a scrub brush from the younger man. The young man glanced at Kameron, who then nodded for him to relinquish a bucket and brush to their master. Without another word, Shihan poured the first bucket of water onto the floor to souse the filth.

The others stood in awe as he fell upon his knees and began to vigorously scrub away the disease and refuse of man.

Silently, each Keeper followed suit and knelt beside their master to scrub away his inherent shame, their own shame, and that of every other human being who walked the earth.

Yum kept the hot water flowing throughout the temple that night, in the cleaning buckets for the inner chamber and for the bathing basins kept in the rooms of the chosen. At times, the only sound that could be heard was the continual pouring of water from the courtyard well into wooden buckets, and hot water being transferred into countless basins and bowls. Shihan had given strict instructions that the unconscious Divinely chosen were not to be disturbed in any way, even as they were being meticulously washed. Each had been thoroughly bathed and made clean and warm with fresh linens for garments and bedclothes upon which to sleep.

Four of the men required several thorough washings throughout the night. The Keepers bustled about in silence or low whispers; none dared to disturb the slumber of the Divine with errant chatter or raised voices. And as dawn broke over the snowcapped mountains of the Tian Shan, the perpetual gardens of Temple Khan Tengri alighted with blooms rarely seen in the world below. And still, the eleven slept and were continuously watched by at least one Keeper. But then fevers set in. Yum, Li and Shihan rushed to each sleeping chamber to observe the men and women as their brows beaded heavily with sweat and their entire bodies became wet with perspiration.

Shihan remained calm, and again instructed that each was to be kept clean and dry at all costs and the linens refreshed as often as necessary. Li began to worry that perhaps some viral sickness was plaguing their charges when the Moshi twins began to have seizures that made their entire bodies quake so violently, he feared their bones might break.

"No, my friend. God is at work here, and He has charged us with keeping His workrooms clean. That is all," Shihan assured the doctor.

"But these fevers, Master, surely their brains will boil in their heads!" Li fretted.

"Li ... there are impurities that cannot be seen with the human eye," explained Shihan. "The Creator is never remiss in His purpose, and it is His intent to purify these bodies and their spirits. And so, it shall be done."

Shihan then placed a reassuring hand on Li's shoulder before turning away to return to the temple's inner chamber to perform one final task.

The sun was already up, and he had sent all but Kameron to their beds less than an hour before. He expected Kameron would not be long in what Shihan had sent him to do.

11

Shihan's Revelation

The next morning, Shihan rose early and went into the atrium of the chamber after looking in on the eleven, who he now fully believed had suffered for the sake of the world. The stench that had pervaded the hallways of the temple the previous night was now completely gone.

Kameron had eventually persuaded him to take his leave and retire upon returning to the chamber the night before. The younger Keeper remained behind to douse the stone floor repeatedly with the cherry blossom oil that Shihan asked him to press from the fresh blooms in the garden. The whole space now smelled like the fresh open air of a spring meadow. The chamber out of which the entities had emerged was now completely empty and stood as dark and silent as any cave. Where the final two sentinels had gone, Shihan didn't know, but they were no longer inside of the chamber.

Yet, he had the distinct feeling they remained within the temple, for there was a peace about the place and amongst the Keepers that he had not expected. A sense of calm as though nothing wholly unexpected had taken place the night before. The old master basked in the quiet serenity of the room and his thoughts began to wander:

Yes ... this space had indeed been occupied by the presence of God, if only for a moment, but now it stands empty and holds naught but the memory of Him.

Whether he was waiting for what he believed would inevitably be the next impending supplicant at the temple gates, or remain endlessly expectant of some new revelation of self from one of the Keepers already in residence, the whole business seemed rather funny.

But why now? Had his entire existence here at the temple been to await the arrival of, care for, and wait alongside those who had been selected by God? And to await the arrival of The Creator Himself or Itself?

How many years and days had he been here? How long ago did he succeed in retraining his mind and body to stop responding to the passage of time? How many Keepers – many of whom he had raised from childhood – had waited with him? He had held close and comforted many in their final waning moments of life, when a person's faith often falters and the terror of having wasted one's precious days upon this Earth begin to scratch at the very soul who is being called to rest. And yet, still he remained ... waiting.

Never in his life had he experienced the physical act of love, nor had he ever recalled fostering or harboring any such desire. None who walked through the gates of the temple did, because once a person made their way onto the grounds of Temple Khan Tengri, all such desires were expunged as if they had never existed. The temple was a place of waiting and preparedness. There were no other needs of the flesh outside of sustenance, except to once again hear the summoning of the Voice that had brought them. Shihan could well imagine a young person in their prime feeling the same giddiness and nervous twinges of excitement in their belly that he was now experiencing for the first time, because now there were Divine Beings in his care and in his Keep.

These were Beings he fully intended to usher into this chaotic physical plane with the same dexterity and care that any good surgeon would when birthing a newborn babe into the world. A rare smile spread broadly across his face and his eyes sparkled with renewed vitality. He allowed the peace he now felt to join with the contentment he always seemed to carry within his spirit. This was his favorite time in his waking hours, the predawn, a time when he imagined every moment that was to come on the new day was preparing itself to be enjoyed at the height of its purpose. In as much as a symphony orchestra prepares to play its first opening notes, he stood with his eyes closed and his hands concealed within the warm sleeves of his kimono.

But then ... he felt a gentle tugging in his spirit.

So distinct was the sensation that it caused him to catch his breath. Shihan kept his eyes closed and reached beyond his physical form with his spirit. He could clearly hear the wind as it made its way over, around and through the many cracks and crevasses of the mountain upon which he lived. He clearly sensed the movement of Kameron somewhere beyond the hallway where he now stood.

Kameron, who was always awake and diligent about his duties at the onset of dawn, had just finished drawing the morning water from the well. He was now moving as silently as a cat through the temple corridors toward the kitchen fires.

But there was something else. Shihan could hear the voice of a man whispering," Come Faithful One." After a moment of silence, the disembodied voice spoke again, "Please come Faithful One."

This time the voice was as clear and present as if the speaker were standing at Shihan's side. He instinctively turned in the direction of the voice, thinking perhaps one of the Keepers needed his help. But he knew it was not so, for he knew the voices of every one of his charges. He knew their intonations and vocal patterns, which were as distinct as a set of fingerprints.

Shihan opened his eyes to find that, as he had suspected, he was quite alone. Again, the voice spoke, "Please Faithful One ... come ... I will speak with you." The elder could almost feel someone or something tugging at his elbow. He turned and began walking down the still quiet corridor of the temple. The voice continued to beckon him, coming to him like a soft, warm breeze on the side of his face. "Faithful One, I will speak with you ... please come."

As he entered the corridor outside the resting chambers of the eleven Divine, the voice became stronger, closer. Shihan could feel himself enveloped in energy. Even though he had walked this same path less than thirty minutes before and looked into each chamber to ensure all was well, he retraced his steps at a steady, unhurried gait, for there was no hurry in him.

He looked in the first chamber and saw Paolo, who, along with the others, was now inhabited by The Iyrin. He was sound asleep on his wooden cot. At the bedside was a low table with a lantern and a single chair occupied by a watchful Keeper. Each room was the same. The Iyrin in their human hosts still slumbered, and upon seeing him once again in the doorway, each Keeper bowed to their master as if this second visit were the first. And still the voice beckoned. Shihan reached the threshold of the eighth chamber and there, the voice fell silent. He had the sudden and unexpected sensation of being released from a loved one's embrace. For the briefest of moments, he felt as though he had entered a vacuum of silence and stillness.

The light of morning had begun its trek across the mountains, and it seeped underneath the single wooden frame of the window in the chamber. It took a moment for the old man's eyes to focus in the changing light, but he was well acquainted with the simple furnishings of the room, which were the same as the other sleep chambers. A wood chair with a burlap seat positioned against the left wall sat directly across from an equally simple but comfortable cot. There was an end table standing close to the head of the bed for convenience. On the table an oil lantern stood dark, a bowl of fresh water, and small swathes of linen with which to bathe and cool the brow of the Divine, as required. On the scrubbed wooden planks of the floor and partially concealed beneath the bed, there was a personal receptacle for nature's call. In the chair a weary Keeper by the name of Michel sat slumped forward with his chin on his chest. His breathing was slow and easy; the olive tones of the flesh just beneath his long eyelashes belied his weariness. Yet, Shihan's unending sense of duty and purpose found no quarter of empathy for the man. His brow furrowed as he formed a thought in his mind. *The man's duty was to...*

Before Shihan could finish his thought, he heard Terris' baritone voice finish it in his head, "... watch over me, and he has done so. It is I who grants him rest."

Shihan's mouth fell agape, as he had not been allowed to complete his thought concerning Michel's reprimand. Not only had his thought been interrupted, it had also been answered for him inside his head! On the small cot surrounded by crisp bed linens woven from blonde alpaca hair sat the countenance of the man who had arrived at The Keep nearly frozen to death a little less than twelve weeks before. He was sitting upright with his back against the modest headboard of the cot. Terris, the Black man from America, had a voice that resonated from the depths of his broad chest. His voice was a deep melodious baritone and could not be disregarded under any circumstance.

This man was created to be heard, thought Shihan. He was as certain of this as he was that the man who lay before him had, without question, heard even this last unspoken thought.

A broad, toothy grin spread across Terris' face, confirming the elder man's suspicions.

"Please do not disturb the young man's rest. I only just managed to put him to sleep a moment or two before you came. And he was very weary." Once gain Terris' voice came to Shihan's mind.

Shihan's gaze fell upon Michel and a single tear expressed from his eye, as his heart unexpectedly swelled with empathy at the sight of the simplistic grace of the sleeping man. He had been made to understand just how much Michel desired to do a good job at whatever was requested of him to make God and his old master proud. But he had indeed been awfully tired after the events of the previous night.

"He is a good man, Divine. It was you who summoned me then?"

"Yes, Faithful One ... it was." Shihan bowed his head and respectfully averted his eyes from that which he now knew was Divine. Terris Jackson had certainly been a formidable man, although he was merely a man with a physique and countenance that defied his fifty-plus years upon the earth – this coupled with the oft-unspoken burden of being a man of color in the ever color-conscious world of men.

But now, this formidable man had merged with the Divine Light of The Creator and had become something more than man. His rich, dark brown skin possessed a preternatural glow and his presence demanded attention and yet, simultaneously, a respectful aversion of direct eye contact from those who were less than what he had become was necessary. It was almost instinctively unavoidable, because a Divine light now inhabited what had been no more than the fleshy mortal coil of a human man less than forty-eight hours before. There was a knowing quite clear, present, and visible behind the eyes of this new creature, a presence that had nothing to hide from anyone who chose to return its gaze.

There was a level of openness and love, acceptance, empathy, pity and purpose, rendered so unabashedly bare that mortal man would find himself unable to maintain his sanity and faculties in the face of such honesty. Shihan's eyes momentarily shut tightly at his brief reminiscence of how unclean and unworthy the species of man had truly become.

"Divine, I will do as you bid."

"Please sit down, I will talk with you." The silent and simple request was more of a merciful plea. Terris calmly gestured toward the foot of his cot. Shihan sat tentatively on the edge of the bed; his trembling hands still concealed within the folds of his robe. So, too, his slightly labored breathing was concealed.

He realized the air had become heavy, as though his body was suddenly trying to process oxygen at a significantly higher altitude. He briefly wondered if there would be even less oxygen available if he moved closer to the Divine being. The notion became a clear truth, which he made note of as his eyes once again fell on the sleeping form of Michel and the dark circles underneath his eyes and his uncharacteristic exhaustion. Could these be the beginning effects of long-term proximity?

"You must have a great many questions to ask of us," Terris stated plainly.

"Yes, Divine – indeed, there is much I would ask, if permitted." Shihan's voice was that of a hopeful youth.

"For what reason do you call me Divine?", Terris genuinely inquired.

"You are that which is both human flesh and the sacred spirit of God. Is that not so?"

"Is that not true of all men? Are you not also flesh and the essence of The Creator?", Terris raised an eyebrow.

"Perhaps ... but I have borne witness to your trials and I say truly you have become more than a man." Shihan said, lowering his gaze respectfully.

"Ah, but alas, no man is ever more than any other man. For then surely, he would be no man, at all ... but something else altogether," said Terris. A kind but knowing smile spread mischievously across Terris' face and his brown eyes glowed with a preternatural golden hue.

"But are you not *something else*? Something ... more?" Shihan spoke cautiously.

"When a man is born, he is as close to completion as he will ever be. His years upon this plane teach him daily that he must separate himself from The Creator. This is the sin of Humankind, and therefore, a man walks this earth separated from the essence of his soul – from the portion of himself that will forever be bound to that which brought it into being. Man lives to fill a void that can be satisfied by only one act. The act of reuniting with the part of himself that is the essence of God. But you, Faithful One, you are far more worthy to be called Divine than my companions or I." A soft golden glow emanated from Terris' eyes as he spoke.

"How can that be?" Shihan asked, his eyes wide with shock, his face flushing bright red.

Terris' quiet tenor gently continued, saying, "The Creator has a purpose for all He has created. I ... we – The Iyrin ... were created with the sole purpose of following the command of that which willed us into being."

Terris continued:

"I have not now, nor have I ever known or desired anything different. I know only the bliss that comes when one is fulfilling their purpose for existence to the fullest. I have never known sadness or regret of self, only joyful contentment.

"Yet you – you were born of man and have lived only in the world of men. A world full of temptation and choice, a world that has succeeded in removing itself so far away from its source that it is now only the soil which has retained its memory and faith in God. And yet you, Faithful One, not only heard but answered a calling few understand. You took the extended hand of The Creator like you were a child and you came to this place, which had been prepared for one such as you. You have lived and accepted this extended life waiting for what – you did not know – nor if or when it was to happen. But here you have remained of your own choosing while cataloguing the many miracles granted you by The Creator.

"And now, more than one hundred and eighteen years have shadowed your brow and for all those years, never once have you given over to the evils of this world, the evils that preoccupy the hearts and minds of many men in this, His once favored world. No, Faithful One, it is you who are truly Divine, and even more so, because you have been so by choice. Do you see and understand now?

"I did not choose to be here in service to The Creator. I am here because I was sent, as is my purpose. But you, my friend, are here because you were invited. You could have said no, as many before you and since you have done. But here you are in service, out of love and of your own free will. And that, Faithful One, is the very definition of divine in the eyes of My Father in Heaven."

As he spoke these words, Terris' eyes glowed brightly and kindly, and he placed a comforting hand on the old man's arm.

Tears rolled freely down Shihan's face, and Terris reached out and grasped the man's small hands lovingly in both of his wide, thickly calloused palms. The fragile and deceptively delicate hands of the older man were completely encompassed by the strong, work-worn hands of the younger man.

"Now, bring to me that which you have coveted from our arrival," his voice was kind, patient and gentle.

"But I have taken nothing," said Shihan, in protest. Who would dare take from these Divine beings?

Terris laughed lightly, as though humoring a small child.

"Faithful Master, he said. "It has always been the way of man to covet and glorify what he does not understand. I speak of the jars you have hidden in the alcove of this very temple. Please bring them to me, for we will have need of what they hold." Terris' eyes remained kind, his face glowing with a knowing light from within.

Again, the shame of his humanity rose within Shihan's throat like a stone. "Oh, but Divine, it is of material most foul."

"And yet, you would preserve this offal to reaffirm your faith?" Terris' voice belied the faintest hint of impatience. He spoke sternly as if requiring a child to justify the soundness of his actions.

"Was I wrong to do so?"

"My Father works goodness and purpose through even the most wretched of things. Even that which one would readily discard serves some function in His design. You were created in, and of, wisdom; you move, as He would have you move. Please bring forth the jars so my companions and I might reclaim that which belonged to the bodies we now inhabit." His voice was once again kind and patient in its tenor.

"I will do as you say, but I have one question." Shihan looked directly at Terris, who nodded in acquiescence. "What of the others ... the ones of whom it is written? Those of your kind who are bound unto the Earth?" Shihan's gaze did not falter from Terris' face as the eyes of The Iyrin, Arch Amun, who now inhabited the man known as Terris, glowed brightly from behind human orbs.

"You speak of The Fallen." Terris' voice was deep and ethereal, as though the man and the actual voice of the Arch Amun were speaking in unison.

The room became still and the very motes of dust in the air ceased to move. Shihan dared not move a muscle as Terris continued.

"We Iyrin are the creations of Our Father, and we are more in number than man's mind can imagine. Yes, there were those, more than two hundred by your count, who followed The First when he fell from Grace. There were those who were disobedient to My Father's will to preserve the Earth for the flowering of Man. And those who would taint Mankind with their seed and with wisdoms that Man was not yet meant to have, for you were My Father's children. Not ours. So yes – some Iyrin did fall – but not all. Not most. Not enough to be but less than a speck in My Father's eye. But now their essence has returned unto the Earth to take their vengeance through Man. This is why we have been sent to watch – for Man will decide his own fate. We are but Watchers."

Shihan was shaking as he bowed his head obediently and rose from the bedside. He found Yum and a female Keeper called "Shamsin" standing in the doorway. The pair openly stared at Terris in awe because the skin on his body appeared almost luminescent in contrast to the cream-colored tunic he wore. Terris nodded kindly in their direction and smiled at them before closing his glowing brown eyes in silent repose. When he did so, some of the brightness in the room seemed to fade.

"Of what does he speak Shihan?" Yum inquired, frightened but always eager to assist.

"Come," Shihan replied simply, as Michel let out a loud snore, having never stirred from his slumber.

Shihan, Yum and Shamsin made their way back into the anteroom of the inner chamber and the dark recessed alcove embedded deep into a wall off to their right. There, Shihan retrieved the first of three bronze trays holding a total of eleven small, ornate, hand-carved jars, each of which had been sealed with candle wax.

"What are these, master?" Shamsin asked.

"Remnants of the waste from their mortal selves. I should have guessed they would see even that which was done in secret. I was alone when I preserved these before the others came in here to clean. I don't mind telling you, it was very unpleasant business," said Shihan quietly.

"But why would you do such a thing?" said Shamsin. He was scowling in disgust.

"And yet, he has asked for them, is this not answer enough?" Yum admonished her gently, as was his way. They carried the jars on trays from the inner chamber, back to Terris' sleeping quarters and left the tray on the table before he instructed them to leave him to rest.

Shortly thereafter, Master Shihan had the outermost doors leading to the inner chamber permanently sealed. The entrance to the chamber itself would remain forever littered with the shattered pieces of the massive broken seal and the two colossal wood doors, which time had turned to stone – doors hewn open by God and sealed shut by God, only to be rendered open and thrust aside by God. There was nothing left for mortal man to do.

12

The Iyrin Called to Earth by God

And behold these are the names of we who passed unto the Earthly realm of Man, through those gates wrought by My Father's hand – and unto the Temple Khan Tengri and placed within the wells and lean-tos of the white covered mountains of the Earth, before the recorded time of Man. And we were thirteen pillars in all. Eight to watch and walk amongst Man, two to cradle and stay the wombs and hearts of the women of the Earth, two who would remain in heavenly form to guard the Holy Gates of God unto the last, and one of whom to be called back unto the Heavenly Hall of The Host.

Amun:

I, Amun, am the oldest of The Iyrin who took on the body of the man once known as "Terris," the Arch by whose name Man has come to affirm his honoring of the Lord. My Father revealed His presence through me to Man in the land of Egypt and the men of that place called me "The Hidden One" in their tongue. I was the first of The Iyrin sent to make God's presence known in the land of Egypt, and then I was called away from the realm of Man back to My Father in Heaven. Before this time, I possessed no name, for my Creator had but to turn His thoughts to me and I was hence.

Bezalel: "In the Shadow of God," walks within the body of Erik and toils under the close protection of God. The Iyrin who learns and records all of the things Mankind has ever written, so in Man's own flesh it will be recalled unto Man in his own tongues in God's time.

Cafziel: "Walks the Earth as Milos," The Iyrin who watches in solitude and keeps account of the tears and of Men who walk the Earth.

Uziel: "The Strength of God," watches over Man as Shylo and is one the seven Iyrin who instilled and maintained the faith in God among Men. One who shall bear the weight of the prayers of Humankind upon Heavenly Winds during the days of judgment.

Ya'Aneh: "Yahweh Will Help," walks as Elisheva, the one who is known among Men as Raphael, the healer of the dying daughter Earth and companion to the hearts of righteous Men. If ever the faith and fortitude of the righteous falter and become like a lamb without a shepherd in the eyes of the evil one who loves man not. In the form of flesh or spirit, by the Grace of The Living God and the blood sacrifice of His Holy Son that yet stains the dust of the Earth. Ya'Aneh and staff will protect thee.

Uriel: The "Fire of God," walks with Gunaar and presides over the clamor and terror to be found in the heavens and upon the Earth. The Iyrin who uplifted the man called "Enoch" throughout his visitations of God's holiest places in those days before the coming of the Lamb. The one who whispers the events yet to come to those who have ears to hear and hearts to understand all that precedes the coming of The Most High.

Mitzrael: "Walks as Paolo," The Iyrin who will bring about obedience within the hierarchies amongst men who have dared use what name of the Lord they will as currency upon the tradesman's table. For those who have profited in this way in the world and seek to hide within the walls of false temples, shall surely find sorrow in the lowliest places beyond the sight of God. Only God shall stand in final judgment of Man.

Sepheriel and Sandelphon: "The Moshi Twins," The Iyrin created in one likeness, one each for the sons and daughters of man. The greatest of us serve as guardians of the wombs of Mankind and stay the quaking hands of women who weep for their children unseen but not lost to the eyes of God.

Omael: "Stands as Yukiro," The Iyrin who would stand with the Twins, Sepheriel and Sandelphon, to stay the spirits of those in mourning and in need of patience. One who will take guardianship of every manner of beast upon the Earth and the souls of the innocent, until such time when God births Humankind anew upon the Earth, and when Omael will usher the head of each and every one through the veil of the womb in their turn.

Sitael: "Seth," one among us who remains unchanged to defend God's Holy Gate until it is melded shut by a mighty blow from Gabriel's sword.

Yomael: The Iyrin who remains as a pillar, unchanged in service to our Father.

Mirzaih: "Walks as Randle," The Iyrin who was once Man, and at whose death whereby there was much suffering and a letting of blood, but he showed such grace, penitence, supplication and purity of life, that he found love and favor in the eyes of The Most High. The Iyrin Mirzaih shall walk as a Man or a Wo-Man amongst Mankind, unbeknownst to all and shall measure the benevolence and piety left in Man. For Mirzaih was born but a man of man and sought out the spirit of God in a world of chaos, as is every man's task in his age.

13

The Arch Michael Speaks on Gabriel

Gabriel was given the most beautiful wings. Mine were
the strongest and Uriel, well, they were certainly
unique but then, I suppose each of us could say the same. But
Gabriel ... there was always something about Gabriel ... The
Creator's favorite.

It is impossible for you to have any idea or understanding
of our relationship with The Father. It is beyond your compre-
hension. Gabriel was indeed the favored one, but this in no
way diminished our value in The Creator's eyes. Gabriel is a
stunning creature. He was skillfully made to be so – his countenance literally stops time, as you understand the concept.

Oh, it is for only a miniscule measurement of what you
understand as time – for only The Father can truly measure time.
But the fact it does happen is one of The Creator's greatest joys!

As for the rest of us, Uriel, Raphael, Uziel, Amun, Bezalel,
Mirzaih, Cafziel, and Omael, we, each of us, have our purpose.
And we were created to fulfill our purpose without judgment,
qualm or question. Our glory is found in being called to our
purpose by The Creator!

14

Amun & Terris Jackson, The Man

Amun had become of one mind with the human who was called "Terris," and could now, therefore, fully understand the arrogance of Man. When Man's consciousness addressed the return of The Father in artistic forms such as paintings, books or in the countless moving pictures they thrived on, it could only be Man's ego that would allow him to believe or contemplate the concept of Divine Beings concerning themselves with the selfishly perceived troubles of Mankind.

There was not now, nor would there ever be, a "war in heaven" over the mere existence of Man. There were no daily battles or debates over Man's innate goodness or deserving grace, or his potential for or a lack of the same. Unfortunately, what the sons and daughters of man had failed to realize over the eons of self-aggrandizement, plagiarism and the contorting of the words that God, in His many forms, had given Man to live by, was that he, Mankind had missed the mark. Man had fallen far short of His Father's expectations of redemption and forgiveness. And with the physical state the Earth was in, the rod could only be stretched so far.

As Amun joined his divine spirit with all that was once a human being named Terris Jackson, his flesh, his thoughts, his desires and everything he had ever been consciously or subconsciously aware of since his conception – all became known to The Iyrin.

Amun was now joined with a species that believed its survival was worth fighting for ... and dying for if need be. Terris' first mental struggle with Amun, and his first transgression, was in thinking his kind would someday come to possess the mental and physical capacity to defy God Himself.

Amun admired the tenacity of men who felt that Humanity was worth much of an effort. And he would gladly cease to exist in the name of whatever The Father deemed worthy of such a sacrifice. Unfortunately, and as of yet unknown to the human race, The Father did not think so. In truth, it would have been merciful for The Creator to swiftly destroy his defiant creation, rather than to subject them to the travails and trials that were yet to come upon them. But Amun doubted his Father would be so inclined to show such mercy. He was far too meticulous and patient for that.

Oh, indeed, the Son of Man would return to gather up His children – who for a time had been His favorite distraction. And gather them He would in such a way that all who had eyes to see, ears to perceive, a heart with which to suffer, and a mind with which to reason, would no longer question, doubt or disguise the existence of God, His Son of Man, or the power of His spirit. All would know and all would turn their unworthy heads away in shame. Amun did not relish in this thought; he fully felt the heart and the very human desires of his host.

Terris Robert Jackson was by no means a great man, but still, he was a wholly human one. A man much the same as any other, with longings that had never been satisfied and dreams that remained unfulfilled. A man who remained saddened by the realization his hopes and desires would never be fulfilled. A man who had done his level best, yet for all intents and purposes still felt in his heart and mind that he had fallen short of the mark. Amun found a perplexed humor in this, for had not the man been handpicked by God Himself to carry the spirit of The Iyrin? The very mold by which his feeble form was created! And there was still so very much left to do in preparation for (and in the name of) The Father in Heaven. For Amun remembered when Man and his kind were new upon the Earth, and he understood the spirits of the Men The Iyrin were now tasked with were not the same as those of old. These were the fractured generations of those whom The Father had brought forth from the dust of the Earth, and into whose hands He had placed the Sacred Words of Life and His Living Law. The Father, in His patience and wisdom, had repeated this many times in many forms over thousands of years in the count of the lives of Men, and in every language and culture upon the living Earth. The message was always the same.

Yet, Man was enraptured by his own image and lust for dominion over other men and all that lay within his sight, including the heavens above him and the life-giving dust of the Earth beneath his lowly feet, which only God in Heaven could command. So hungry were they to stand as an equal to The Almighty, that most, too many, had lost sight of My Father altogether.

Yes, there was indeed much for Amun and this body, and the inherently ungrateful spirit of this man to do and learn before the soul once known as Terris Jackson, of this dying planet Earth, was finally snatched up to meet its maker. But until such time, Amun would lovingly swaddle Terris' soul within the soft folds of the six wings of The Iyrin unseen. And hold it there safe for all eternity, if need be, or until The Father or the Blessed Lamb bid it surrendered.

15

Yum Speaks With The Divine

Three days following the arrival of The Iyrin, Yum and the young Keeper, Michel, delivered warm broth and fresh linen garments to each in their sleeping quarters, where they had remained confined since their transformation. Terris' quarters were the last of the eleven, and the men found the door of the room propped open and welcoming. Terris was standing motionless near the small window. He was looking out over the mountain peaks in the same manner as all the other eleven transformed men and women had been when Yum and Michel arrived at their doors. He, just like the others, was standing so still he could have been mistaken for a statue. But, both Yum and Michel instinctively felt something different as they took a tentative step over the threshold into this room. Their intent had been to simply leave the clothing and refreshment, which had both been placed upon a serving tray, on the soft padding of the bed and depart without disturbing their guest. But, as soon as they entered the room, both Yum and Michel felt like they had stepped into a vacuum. Yum just happened to be in the process of inhaling through his nose when suddenly, he found he could no longer do so. It was as though he had walked right into the center of a giant glob of translucent jelly, which completely enveloped him.

What little air his nostrils managed to grasp was trapped in the space between the back of his throat and the top of his lungs.

He felt the normally imperceptible movements of the organs
in his body, with the exception of his heart, which had come
to a sudden and slightly painful halt. Then, his heart pumped
exactly one time and it stopped, too. But before Yum's brain
could work out exactly what might be happening and whether
or not time as he understood it could have actually somehow
been suspended in the room in which he was now standing,
Terris calmly turned toward Yum and Michel. In an instant, all
returned to normal and the air was fresh and breathable again.
Michel's youthful and frightened eyes, however, remained
nearly bugged out of his head in shock and confusion. Neither
Keeper said a word about what had just transpired; both only
inhaled and exhaled gratefully, as Terris thanked them warmly
for the tea and expertly woven garments. Yum took particular
notice of the man's countenance and knew it was now much
improved. His skin had a healthy glow to it and was taut against
his ample muscles and skeletal structure. He now completely
belied the half-century or so that he had walked upon the earth
– he looked to be less than thirty-five years old and basking in
the prime of his life. Could it be possible the man had gotten
younger in the days that had just passed?

And yet, the cloudy blindness afflicting his right eye
remained. The left eye was clear and vibrant, and it sparkled
with sharp undeniable focus.

Yum felt that were he to take a closer, deeper glimpse into
the left orb, he might very well be driven mad by whatever
revelations he would see within. It was a far cry, and in stark
contrast to, the milky film of scar tissue and silicone clouding
its partner, thus effectively hiding it from others. When Li first
examined Terris' afflicted eye, he noted the orb dutifully moved
in sync with its counterpart. It mimicked the motions of sight
even though it did not see. Yum looked upon this transformed
man, this soul, as an unfinished piece of art.

Terris smiled kindly at the old man and said, "Is there something you wish to ask of me?"

Yum became aware of his wayward thoughts and said, "I do not wish to seem impertinent."

"The only thing you seem to be is curious. What do you wish to know?" Terris' voice was as kind and warm as an evening summer breeze.

"For any who knew you before, none could now deny that your countenance truly has been transformed. It seems every affliction in your wholly mortal body has been purged from you. All, it would seem, save ..." Yum quietly replied and humbly gestured toward Terris' cloudy right eye.

"Ah, yes, my eye," Terris retorted, with a smirk on his mouth.

"But surely you can see from it, Divine. Surely, its appearance is meant to deceive your enemies," offered Michel, whose tongue apparently only occasionally broke the silence that only minutes before it had been instructed to keep.

Yum gently placed a quelling hand upon the young man's shoulder. The deep, rumbling sound of Terris' laughter emerged from his broad chest like the eruption of a long, dormant vent. The sound swelled within the tiny chamber and rattled the shutters and walls.

The sound and its subsequent effect startled the Keepers, and they behaved like two frightened children. The power of God lay even within the sound of Terris' laughter.

"My friend, I tell you truly, The Creator is no deceiver. I assure you I am as sightless in the eye as I appear to be," Terris said with a wide grin.

"But were you not made whole?" Yum spoke with the high-pitched inquisitiveness of a child.

Terris sensed the uncertainty of the man and knew the very foundations of the old man's faith had been touched. So many of Mankind were desperate to have their feeble understanding of the Divine verified. When it was not, they quaked to the very core of their being. It was to Terris a most pitiful truth, for The Creator did not ask for Man's understanding, merely his belief.

"Perhaps it would be more appropriate to say my human self was indeed fortified in those moments you witnessed. My sight was taken from me by the splintered fragments of a bullet some nineteen years ago," Terris confessed, as he respectfully tasted the tea.

"You were shot?" Michel could no longer contain his natural curiosity and wonder; after all, he was conversing with the Divine. The boy could see no reason for Terris' tale to be any less remarkable than the tales he himself would have to relate one day about the most wondrous events he and the other Keepers had witnessed.

"Michel …!" Yum spoke firmly, but with his usual patience. Terris raised a hand to halt the chiding.

"It is all right, Yum. Yes, there was a group of men having a rather heated argument near a building I was working on. Oddly, or perhaps appropriately enough, construction was my given trade. Eventually, the debate escalated and someone fired a gun. A single shot. I was struck in the eye by a ricocheting fragment of that bullet after it hit a brick wall."

The story Terris told was straightforward and simply put. Without a trace of regret or remorse, he continued. "And until two nights ago, it absolutely the worst pain I have ever known. It took eight surgeries to save what remained of my eye. There was never any hope of my sight being restored, and I was in excruciating pain every single day."

"What did you do?" Again, Michel spoke. But this time, Yum did not protest.

"What did I do?" Terris set his good eye keenly and unwavering upon the young man, and Michel lowered his head and gaze respectfully. Yum sensed a sudden and jarring stillness overtaking the room in that moment; it was full of expectant words of wisdom from the Divine. And then, just as quickly as it had come, it was gone.

"I did what any mortal man would do. I cried. I screamed. I felt sorry for myself, and then I did the most unholiest of all things. I cursed my Creator and lashed out at every living thing that crossed my path. People, animals, plants – it didn't matter. I even considered gauging out my other eye. I raged, Michel ... I raged!"

Terris took the young man by the shoulders and bared his teeth as he spoke this last sentence. Until then, his answer had been quiet, focused, but intensely soft-spoken. Michel's gaze remained downcast, and his whole body reverberated from the unseen power emanating from the hands of the Divine upon his shoulders.

Terris hesitated for a long moment and then seemed to lift the boy's head using only his words.

"But then, young man ... I lived. I learned how to breathe in order to control the pain. I worked better and harder so as not to be seen as a disabled man. In doing so, my work became the work of a true craftsman, who pays the utmost attention to the smallest details of his work and in the work done by others.

The martial arts training I honed as a child became even more of a significant part of my life. Because I had experienced so much pain with my injury, not allowing anyone to get close enough to hit me in my eye became my entire fighting strategy. I was more aware, more alert, faster and sharper."

He continued. "After a while, I discovered I could actually hear my opponent breathing. Anyone who assumed I was at a disadvantage because of my eye would soon be sorely and regrettably mistaken. The lack of sight in one eye was all it took for me to become a better human being, a useful tool in the hand of The Creator, and in the world of men. That which was seen as my affliction would become my salvation. It wasn't until I lost my sight that I became worthy of the task The Creator had intended me for."

"You mean intended for you?" Michel spoke hastily but assuredly in his correction. "You said, 'intended me for' instead of 'intended for me'."

"Forgive his impudence, Divine; he strives to instruct us all on one account or another." Yum sternly tugged at the sleeve of Michel's robe, feeling they had definitely overstayed their welcome.

Terris casually took a few steps back over to where he had been standing by the window. He gazed once again out over the vastness of the sky and the mountains – his eyes were opened wide like the eyes of a bird, seemingly unbothered by the direct sunlight.

Yum observed him and suspected that he was seeing something far beyond the sights of mortal men. And there was another feeling, one that was much more uneasy, but he couldn't quite put his finger on it.

Terris began to speak just as Yum's mind tried to focus on what exactly might be causing his uneasy feeling.

"I am quite aware of what I said, and it was meant to be said thus. Understand that none of us were created nor do we exist to be serviced, but only to serve. Man was created to be a steward to the Earth. This body, Terris, was created and intended for this purpose and that which is yet to come. Just as we, The Iyrin, were created and intended solely for the purpose of doing our Father's bidding."

He spoke as though his thoughts were somewhere very far away, and without so much as a hint of pride or self-aggrandizement, but rather as a plainly stated, inarguable matter of fact. And yet, the lilt of honor was in his voice, for he was Iyrin, the very first of God's creations.

"We are nearby should you need anything," Yum said, with some discomfort, as he urged Michel out of the room.

"Yum, just a moment, I have something for you." Terris' voice was suddenly vibrant and urgent as he turned on his heels. Before Yum could register the fact that he was being spoken to, Terris had reached over to the small table nearest the window and unfolded a piece of cloth.

"Here, I am told you will know what to do with these," he said to Yum confidently.

Yum tentatively approached Terris and looked down into the cloth he was holding in the palm of one large hand. Inside were eleven iridescent stones with hues that varied in the sunlight from red to blue, green, yellow, brown, and several colors Yum could not name and wasn't quite certain he had ever seen before.

"But, Divine, what am I to do with them?" Yum asked, completely perplexed.

"As I said, I have been told that you will know. Have patience. And faith," Terris answered kindly and confidently before rewrapping the cloth and handing the bundle over to Yum. He then turned his attention quietly back toward the window without uttering another word.

16

The Vatican Gardens

Father Josef's heavy brows furrowed deeply when he heard and felt his left hip joint pop loudly and painfully in protest as he repositioned himself on the overly soft cushion of his favorite high-backed armchair. He had been sitting in it for the better part of the evening, and the hours had not been kind to his rheumatic hips. He exhaled wearily while extending one arthritic hand out past a dimly lit floor lamp toward the wood end table standing just to the right of where he sat.

The bulbous knuckles on the backside of his hand inadvertently brushed against the bottle of Stauning he had placed upon the little table, still full and unopened less than five hours ago, but which was now almost empty. The gold insignia ring he wore on his little finger made the tiniest pinging noise as it hit the bottle. The sound made him wonder if this is what's meant when referring to being able to "hear a pin drop." He sighed heavily again and toyed with the idea of topping off the crystal tumbler sitting next to the whiskey, which remained almost a quarter full of the amber liquid. The old priest wondered whether he absolutely needed to top off the glass to help muster up the strength to do what he knew he eventually could not avoid. Josef forced his gnarled fingers to move beyond both the bottle and the glass until he reached the farthest edge of the table.

There, he retrieved several neatly typed pieces of paper and a folded newspaper clipping that lay with them. They had been sent to him in a rather crudely formed white envelope, in care of the private residence of a long deceased relative, whose family ran a modest goat farm just outside Rome.

It was a letter that should have never found him, a man who had been living in self-imposed exile for almost twenty years in one of the most revered places on earth – Vatican City. And while The Vatican was notorious for having innumerable scrutinizing eyes, when it came to their incoming and outgoing mail, they seemed to take little interest in the comings and goings of a heavyset, middle-aged woman delivering a quart of fresh goat's milk to an elderly priest, who was known to suffer from occasional stomach ulcers.

Josef had never met Marcella, a woman he was related to by way of some great marital distance. And who, at the behest of her husband, had delivered both the milk and the rather ominous, bulky envelope directly to his doorstep. Marcella was a kind, round-faced, soft-spoken woman in her mid-forties, whose uncle-in-law, Emil, had been Josef's distant cousin by marriage. But Emil's and Josef's parents had been close, and the boys had grown up together, and despite Josef being four years younger, had remained close friends and confidants until Emil succumbed to lung cancer at the age of forty-five in the fall of 1992.

Emil was not a Catholic, but Josef offered penance on his behalf and lay prostrate before the cross in prayer for seven days and nights to beg God for mercy on his cousin's immortal soul. He believed Emil was a good man because the last words he said to Josef over the phone less than a week before his death were, "Had it not been for you cousin, God certainly never would have found me." Those words rang in Josef's ears for many weeks afterward.

In fact, it had originally been Emil's wife, Claudia, who suggested he retain some sense of privacy after the church called Josef, who was naturally reclusive, into public service.

And Emil, thinking the idea was a sound one, offered the use of his family farm's address for any personal correspondence Josef might wish to engage in, should the need ever arise. But Josef's heart and devotion had always been entrenched in service to God and the church, and in his sixty plus years as a man of the cloth, he had never found it necessary to take his cousin up on the offer, no matter how kindly intended.

At least this is what he believed up until a little over five hours ago, when he unexpectedly found himself staring down at his name, neatly typed in black ink, across the middle of a well-traveled envelope with a blue Brazilian postmark in the upper right-hand corner.

After the portly Marcella made her overly polite departure – rife with the usual perfunctory gestures of the devout – Father Josef closed the door of his modest villa.

His eighty-year-old eyes stared at the envelope with his head cocked slightly to one side as he scratched thoughtfully at one unshaven cheek with his neatly trimmed fingernails. His brain stuttered at first, like one of those old Ford motorcars, and being the methodical man that he was, he didn't tear away at the envelope right away to see what it contained. Somehow, he felt like it would be cheating. He wanted to remember – the where, the how, and who had addressed this mysterious letter to him. Who could have gotten such personal information after all these years?

He stared at the postmark again, this time for a good, long while. "Rio De Janeiro," it read. Slowly, the murky fog that often drifted in wispy patches down the long, narrow lanes of his memory began to shift and clear, for they never fully lifted anymore. And then it began to come back to him, and he remembered hastily giving out the information to a young seminarian many, many years ago.

It was on the last day of a two-week lecture series he was giving at a seminary just outside of Rio. Josef remembered being hurried at the time, literally being pushed into a car that was heading for the airport. A young man asked if he could remain in contact to seek guidance about something, but about what, he could not recall.

For some reason, Josef had responded to the student without hesitation, uttering the name of the tiny farm, or at least what he thought was the name because he had never bothered to set it to memory. This much he did know. He also knew that had been the only instance in which he had ever mentioned the name of the farm to anyone. Because he honestly couldn't remember the place ever crossing his mind since the day his cousin mentioned it to him over forty years ago.

The old priest was pleased with himself because he was fairly certain he had solved the bulk of the mystery behind this most unexpected delivery all on his own. He gingerly opened the envelope without putting any additional mental energy into remembering more of the details from that day in Brazil so long ago. After all, he truly was a humble man of God, and he only hoped that whomever had written to him after all this time had found their way in the world, a way in which to do good works in the name of the Lord. Thus, was the goodness and simplicity of Father Josef's heart.

After reading through the first few pages of the letter, he was compelled to refer to the clipping from *The Rio Times* newspaper, and when he finally read the last page of the letter, his mouth snapped shut with an audible popping sound. Josef's hands trembled uncontrollably, and he strained to focus his eyes, which had overflowed with tears as he strained to look at the wavering letters typed at the very bottom of the final page. He stared in wonder and absolute disbelief at the words of the closing line and the boldly written signature scribbled beneath them.

> "Had it not been for you, I would have never found my way to God."
>
> - *Emil D. Azevedo, MD*

Josef's mouth became as dry as a basket of dead leaves, his legs buckled, and the old priest wobbled to his knees. The pages of the letter, as far as Josef was concerned, had been sent by way of either God or the Devil. The pages were now crumpled between the bulging knuckles of his ill-fitting, interlocked arthritic fingers, which had come up instinctively beneath Josef's chin just as he began whispering fervent prayers in ancient Aramaic.

And there Josef remained, on his knees in prayer until the shock of seeing Emil's name and his dying words – thirty-five years after his death – written across the bottom of a letter that had been mailed only a week before subsided.

He remained on his knees until he was quite certain he could once again look at the last of those pieces of paper and know it was indeed a message to him from his God in heaven, to whom he had devoted the lion's share of his life.

Father Josef stayed on the hard wooden floor in prayer until he could no longer feel his knees, nor sense the tiny cottage in which he had voluntarily sequestered himself from the rest of the world nearly twenty years before.

He prayed until his mind and spirit became as focused as a single beam of light, in order to prepare his mind and body to get the truth he required before leaving his little cottage for what he knew might be the last time.

Once Josef's mind cleared and his nerves had settled a bit, he gathered up the letter and the news clipping and dragged his numb legs and overwrought body into the high-backed armchair with its too soft cushion. It had been given to him many years before by an Egyptian businessman trying to buy his salvation from the church.

After five and half hours has passed, he set the letter and the news clipping aside and reached into the little cupboard built into the wall just behind the armchair to retrieve and open the bottle of whiskey. Josef had intended to save it as a final parting gift for those who were kind enough to pay their respects at the private wake the church would have at the time of his passing.

He was a man of modest means and the few material items he owned would most likely revert back to the church, so Josef thought a toast was the least he could offer. Current circumstances being what they were, the Father filled one of the six exquisitely cut, crystal tumblers. They had also been gifted to him from the same aristocrat in Denmark who gave him the whiskey. Josef downed the liquid without savoring the flavor or feeling the burn of the finely aged spirit, a trick he learned as a much younger man while serving in the military.

He wasn't a habitual drinker, far from it. He was a binging savant, which he had discovered fifty-six years previously, the night before he was to take the most important exam of his life, one that would ultimately solidify and define the foundation of his service to God in the eyes of the church. In a final act of youthful indecision and rebellion, Josef escaped the confines of the seminary, which had been locked down prior to evening prayers. He made his way to the nearest village and preceded to drink every ounce of liquor he could get his hands on. He had always been able to hold his liquor when he was in the military, and he often used this "talent" to swindle money from others.

But on this particular night, after three hours of heavy drinking, not only did he not get drunk, his head cleared, his spirit settled, and his theological thoughts began to go far beyond those of a fifth-year seminarian.

At one point, Josef gazed up into the clear night sky and his vision was transported beyond the sight of the constellations and into the vastness of space. He stood transfixed at the sight of the countless galaxies, which brought forth tears from his eyes, and he felt his consciousness touched and expanded by the spirit of the living God.

Josef had been allowed a mere glimpse of how the Lord could move, and he had wept, not intoxicated, but fully aware. By the time he made it back inside the seminary, it was the height of Grand Silence within, and the entire school was as quiet as a tomb. The only sound to be heard was that of the alcohol sloshing in Josef's belly as he made his way down the dark stone corridors to the students' library.

Josef felt compelled to proceed forward, like he was floating in a dream. Once inside the vast room, he approached the five domineering tiered wooden shelves of aging and dusty theological volumes filling every square foot of the library, accompanied by long reading tables placed in the center of the room. He began pulling several of the books he needed from various shelves, finding them easily despite the semi-darkness of the room. The only source of light was the thin beams of moonlight streaming in from two narrow, rectangular windows at the uppermost portion of the East wall. When Josef finally sat down an hour later, he was surrounded by more than fifty books and maps, the Torah, and the Canons of the Apostles and the Catholic Church. He read and effortlessly retained all that was required for him to pass both the written and oral portions of the final theological exam he was to take four hours later. Everything he looked at seeped into him and was absorbed, like his brain was a sponge. From this time forward, he could recall everything he had seen and read that night. It was the night he learned to read, write and pray in the ancient language of Christ.

Afterward, Josef dutifully confessed to the bishop, did his penance, and vowed never to touch a drop of hard liquor again. Nonetheless, and to the chagrin of some within the church, he was ordained shortly thereafter. Josef had honored his promise, and with the exception of the wine he sipped during the Eucharistic Sacrifice, he had remained to his word and his vows. To Josef's relief, the wine had no effect on his disposition whatsoever, until he read the last page of the mysterious letter and was driven to his knees in prayer by the words written thereon. He knew what he had to do. Father Josef knew that to coax his unconscious mind to find the answers his conscious mind was unable to give, he was going to need a drink.

And so, he settled himself into a deep curve in the cushion of his armchair, a curve created by years of late-night reading and the sleeplessness that comes with old age. With one hand trembling slightly, he refilled the heavy crystal tumbler to the brim with whiskey and raised the glass to his lips. The priest took a long, steady and continuous draught until the glass was empty, this time feeling every bite of the liquor and its warmth as it went down. It wasn't an unpleasant feeling, but rather akin to welcoming an old friend back into your home.

Josef then carefully straightened out the pages of the letter and the news clipping without reading a word of either, until each looked almost as pristine as when they were first pulled from the envelope. He refilled the tumbler and emptied it in the same fashion a third time before he finally began to feel the mental fog, which had long ago become his constant companion, start to lift and fade from his mind.

His vision began to clear and the colors within the room sharper and brighter, deeper and more alive.

He could clearly make out the numerous titles of the books lining his bookshelves, and those standing in stacks of varying heights around his modest sitting room.

He felt his spirit expand, but at the same time he became serene, as if he was slipping into a meditative state. His breathing became measured; he felt wholly disconnected from his body' and time seemed to grind to a halt. He was then moved by an impulse, some inner voice that directed him to retrieve the pages of the letter from the table.

The Father's hands did not tremble one iota as they held up the pages of the letter to eyes no longer completely his own. Eyes that began reading the neatly typed words for the first time:

07 July 2023
Eminence,

May this letter find you in good health and in the blessed grace of our Lord. I beg you forgive the intrusion on your solitude, but after days of reflection, I could think of no other to whom to entrust information I believe was given to me by Providence. I hold little hope of your recalling our brief encounter at the Seminary of St. Joseph in Rio De Janeiro in 2007. At that time, I was a shamefully arrogant student who dared step far beyond his station and approached your person to request a means by which to contact you in future. My dilemma was whether to remain upon the path of ordination or answer the call to become a physician. You, sir, were kind enough to pause long enough to impart upon me (I believed then, as I do know, truthfully) the address to which I have posted this letter, in faith it will find you.

I have never forgotten the words you spoke: "Caseificio Sensi. Ora vai e di 'al monsignore il lavoro che Dio ha riservato per te."

And I confess to you here, as I did to the monsignor immediately following your departure, that our entire encounter was based on a ruse. It was a crude attempt to rise to a challenge put forth by my fellows, as none believed I would approach you in front of the Monsignor or the Papal guests. Only I—and I alone, knew I could and would because I had already made up my mind to confront both my family and the church with my decision to leave St. Joseph's to earn a medical degree.

Your words, Father, served as a sharp reminder that I, a foolish and impertinent deceiver, was unable to hide from He who sees into the hearts of all men.

As to the purpose of this letter and the enclosed news clipping, you are perhaps already aware of the recent reported sighting of Our Lady and a helicopter crash here in Rio on the morning of Thursday, 19 April, atop the Christ the Redeemer monument? The clipping contains an interview given by one of four eyewitnesses, a night watchman named "Alaric Dixon, "and photographic evidence of the alleged aftereffects suffered by him.

The other witnesses are a Ms. Anit Chima, the helicopter pilot, Mr. Daniel Garcia, a television news producer and Mr. Herman Rivera, a news cameraman. All three are employed by Rede Globo, the largest news outlet in South America. While I cannot personally vouch for any of them concerning this matter, after calling in several favors I can attest to their work records. Each are considered well-respected professionals in their chosen fields, and Mr. Dixon has worked at the monument for a little over eight years. He is also the first cousin of Mr. Garcia.

On the night of the incident, Mr. Dixon stated he had stepped outside of his guard's booth for a cigarette when he felt what he believed was rain falling on his forehead and down the front of his shirt. But when he wiped the moisture off his forehead, he saw blood on his fingers and this is what prompted him to look up.

He claims to have seen a young woman dressed in a white garment, fully illuminated by the floodlights of the monument, standing on the outstretched right arm of the statue. Mr. Dixon used his mobile phone to call Mr. Garcia, who had previously promised to compensate him for any firsthand news he might come across.

Mr. Dixon would call the police to report the woman approximately twelve minutes later, but by the time this happened, Mr. Garcia and his crew had arrived at the site and placed their own call to emergency services, and they also reported the woman.

With regard to the helicopter crash, Mr. Dixon told reporters at the scene that he actually witnessed the young woman step out into the empty space between her and the front end of the helicopter, and then step onto the nose of the machine! There was a bright flash of light, which made him shield his eyes with one arm. And when he was able to look again, he saw — and Father, this is a direct quote—"The lady stood on the nose of the helicopter as it went down. It spiraled downward, until the blades hit the side of the hill."

The helicopter went down in the brush, and Mr. Dixon stated a glowing light "like a star" rose from the crash site and floated up into the sky and then disappeared. The next thing he remembers are rescue units and the police helping him get up to his feet from off the ground where he had fainted.

Mr. Dixon refused additional medical attention that night, but once home, he realized he was unable to wash away the aforementioned blood from his forehead and chest.

In an interview given in the presence of his clergyman on 20 April, he stated that neither soap and water, nor diluted bleach could fade the stains.

I will leave it to you to interpret the shapes of those markings on his chest and forehead. According to official reports, no woman (living or deceased) was found at or near the statue at the time of the reported incident.

And here is where I come to play a minor part in these remarkable happenings, as the crash was not a fatal one; the three occupants of the helicopter were all transported to Hospital Adventista Silvestre, where I work as a senior general internist. I was not on call the night of the incident, and I did not speak to, nor did I consult with any of the victims. It was, however, remarked throughout the hospital how incredibly lucky they all were not to have been more severely injured given the severity of the circumstances under which they were admitted. News of how the trio survived the mangled and twisted metal of the completely unrecognizable helicopter on the side of the mountain would be in the local newspapers for days following the incident. The producer, Mr. Garcia, was observed for less than twenty-four hours and released the following morning.

It was notated in his record that he was quite agitated and ranting about not being able to find some digital recordings that were supposedly taken during his flight over the statue. He never mentioned the young woman, however, he just ranted on and on about the missing video footage. Attending physicians attributed his behavior to stress and shock, and of course, treated him accordingly.

Mr. Garcia's verbal accusations and suspicions against the authorities continued the next morning and up until his release. He was careful never to say exactly what those recordings were supposed to have captured.

And he seemed convinced the authorities had either lost or confiscated them, because nothing could be found in the few personal belongings salvaged from the crash site and brought to the hospital. His last known destination was the police station to find out if investigators had retrieved anything else from the wreckage.

That station was the last place Daniel Garcia was seen alive; two days later he was found dead in his home from causes, as of yet, officially undeclared. And even though he was not a practicing Catholic, the church has claimed his remains for burial, as his deceased mother listed his name on the registry when he was a child. The cameraman, Herman Rivera, was brought in virtually, and some might even say "miraculously" unscathed. Although his mental state was reported to be akin to catatonic shock, he had no concerning outward physical injuries notated in his medical file.

Mr. Rivera's response to physical stimuli was almost non-existent, and his speech remained limited to a repetitive litany of Hail Mary. His treatment plan was simple; keep him in hospital for a complete psychiatric evaluation, with a hopeful outlook of a full recovery from the shock of the accident. The pilot, Ms. Chima, was notated to be a healthy female in her early thirties, whose injuries, such as they were, would have to be considered the worst of the three.

Although again, not feared permanent or life threatening, she'd suffered the equivalent of second-degree burns to her upper facial area.

They appeared, however, very similar to radiation burns rather than those suffered from U-V light exposure or powder burns. The resulting effect was a remarkable dilation of her right pupil to an unusually large degree.

Again, it was an issue the attending physician, Dr. Mark Bringleson, felt would eventually correct itself with mild treatment and the passage of time.

My shift at the hospital began the following afternoon, the day after the trio was admitted, and as it was my habit to visit the hospital chapel before attending patients, I did so on that evening.

When I entered the chapel, it appeared empty as I expected, but as I knelt in prayer, I heard a woeful weeping and a mumbling sound. I looked around, thinking perhaps it was a frightened child but found to my utter shock a fellow doctor, who I have mentioned before, Dr. Mark Bringleson. He was curled in a ball, hiding underneath the altar and mumbling what sounded to me like a random set of numbers: 6...1...0...4...6...1...6. ..1...4...9...3.

The man was shaking so violently, he had wet himself. And I was too terrified to move him from where he lay, fearing he had either suffered a stroke or some mental break. He must have read as much on my face, because he suddenly reached out with hands curled like talons and hooked both my wrists in his claw-like fingers. He held me with such a grip, as though I was a life raft and he was drowning beneath the waters of the sea. I could not begin to fathom what was going on. That's when I saw the raw desperation and regret ... yes, Father, regret, in his eyes. I must tell you that I knew this man to some degree. We worked together for over a decade, and he was someone whom I considered a friend. He was a good doctor with a level head.

His worst flaw to date, as far as I know, was a rather rough bout with midlife, having perhaps gone a bit overboard to impress a woman who was a little less than half his age. He began sobbing uncontrollably, and I offered to get something to help calm him down; in truth, he frightened me. I realized then that whatever was going on, it was not stroke, but the ravings of a maniac, one who happened to have a death grip on me. But he was also a fellow doctor, and at the moment, my patient, and I knew he'd scream in terror if I spoke of leaving him. So, I told him to calm down and tell me what had upset him so badly.

With spittle dribbling down the corners of his mouth, he began by telling me that he had been on call earlier that morning and had randomly been assigned to minister to Ms. Chima, who had been brought in the evening before. But what he witnessed while examining her eyes put him in fear of his life and everlasting soul. He told me his mind simply could not make sense of what he had seen inside of the woman's head. He said he had never been so terrified in his life as he was in the room with her.

Eminence, Dr. Bringleson stated to me that when he looked into the pupil of Anit Chima's right eye, he clearly saw within its depths an animated replica or image (this is all I can think to call it) of our known galaxy, the Milky Way in its entirety. As if one were approaching it from outside of our known galaxy—from "above and beyond it" were his exact words. The arms of the galaxy were spinning counter-clockwise and from this perspective he also bore witness to five winged Beings of Light surrounding a sixth, which traveled in the center of them and bore the Holy Mother on its back.

He said she wore a white tunic and a blue veil that shone. He could see her brown hair and slight curls around her face. He wept while describing her and it seemed to calm him somewhat. He also said that directly ahead of the center winged being bearing The Lady, there was a seventh, which he described as the leader.

And then The Lady turned and looked directly into the face of my friend the doctor and smiled warmly at him. The winged being in the rear of the group and to the left of The Lady, turned its head and looked over its shoulder at my friend, at which point he heard these words inside of his head: "The blood returns. Prepare, as Man did not heed The Lord before."

And then, in what was perhaps the most fantastic thing I have ever heard from the mouth of a man who only a day prior I would have sworn was sober and sane ... Dr. Bringleson told me a beam of light emanated from the right eye of his patient and projected itself across the room!

After speaking, he fell unconscious as if from the sheer exhaustion of having told the tale. Fearing the worst, I checked his vital signs, only to find his heart barely beating at an unbelievable rate of twenty-four beats per minute. He had fallen into a coma — from which he would fully recover six days later with absolutely no memory of having ever examined Ms. Chima or of speaking to me in the chapel.

And yes, at the time, I also thought my colleague was most assuredly mentally afflicted, until I personally witnessed the mayhem that ensued in the hospital less than three hours after he relayed his fantastic story to me. I was on my way to see Ms. Chima for myself, but when I stepped into the hospital ward, the place was in total disarray!

Both she and the cameraman, Mr. Rivera, who was reported to be catatonic, had somehow managed to leave the hospital without anyone having taking notice of either of them! I looked in each of their rooms and in Mr. Rivera's, I found his clothes were missing and, by all accounts, he seemed to have left of his own volition.

I also took the liberty of reviewing his medical notes and found that he, too, had been repeating a series of numbers, just as my friend had when I found him in the chapel. They were similar numbers, only the attending nurse had apparently managed to record an entire sequence of them: "161014693227," because Mr. Rivera had repeated them over and over at the end of each one of his Hail Mary recitations.

It was concluded that both were simply the last hapless thoughts the man had prior to the crash and the effects of the shock he suffered from the resulting trauma. But Dr. Brigleson's name was nowhere in Mr. Rivera's records, so why would they both be repeating similar numbers?

Then. I went to Ms. Chima's room. As you can well imagine, the most fantastic element of what my friend told me was the iridescent beam of light or "glow" he claimed he saw emerge from her eye. Sir, I tell you, I honestly didn't believe a word of it, but something compelled me to investigate. I walked into the room, which was already in the process of being prepped for the next patient, I looked closely at the wall across from the foot of the bed where he had examined her. There, on the wall, at a height of approximately two and half meters, I found a reddish-brown oily substance. I took several pictures of it with my phone, and then I turned off the lights. I could see clearly the spot had an almost imperceptible white glow about it.

It could have very well been my imagination, and I am hesitant to mention it, but still, I must, because I feel it is important to be completely frank with you on the matter. I took another photo with my phone, but got nothing but bright white, overexposed blotches on both. By the morning of 21 April, the local news was reporting on nothing else but the crash and Mr. Dixon's newly released eyewitness testimony.

Daylight aerial video aired on every news station showing the wrist of the Redeemer statue where the mysterious woman had supposedly stood. Even at a distance, one could clearly see the wrist was covered with an ochre-colored liquid, which was somehow flowing freely and by all appearances, quite heavily, from some unseen source. It dripped into the palm and off the monument as if ... and I have no other way of saying this, but as if from an open vein.

Given the size of the edifice ... well, I am sure I need not elaborate further; you can imagine how disturbing a sight it was for the faithful. The substance, of course, was eventually tested and found to be human blood. However, I am not privy as to the type or the DNA results, or even as to whether such tests were run. And I cannot begin to imagine where such an amount of human blood could be procured and to what lengths anyone would have to go to prevent it from coagulating under those conditions.

Church officials immediately stepped in and had the offensive sight draped from public view while both police, and I imagine, church investigations continued.

News of the event has since been pulled from the local television and print outlets. I have it on good authority that the church has ordered that no further mention of the subject is to be made during Mass regarding the possibility of whether a Marian appearance occurred at the monument.

At some point following the interview he gave to the newspapers on 20 April, Mr. Dixon was taken into seclusion by either his family or the church; I cannot say for not certain which. As I stated, after six days, Dr. Bringleson made a full recovery and then unexpectedly resigned from his post at the hospital. And without a word to anyone, he abandoned his home, left all his personal belongings behind, and disappeared. No one has seen or heard from him in over three months. Yet, I am certain you might be privy to this information as well, for it is known that investigators from the Vatican came here wanting to speak with him regarding his contact with Ms. Chima. I briefly spoke with them myself, once they found out that I was the first person to speak with him after he fled her bedside. But I told them none of what I write to you now, and to my knowledge, the church has yet to locate him.

Eminence, there is one final point — the homes of Daniel Garcia and Herman Rivera were both ransacked by persons unknown. And I believe that perhaps Mr. Garcia and his colleagues did, in fact, record something significant from the cockpit of the helicopter. Something significant happened on the statue that night.

It was recorded and someone is looking for those recordings. Two days ago, I received an envelope addressed to me at the hospital. Inside was a sheet of paper with handwritten numbers on it — 1610145693227. At the bottom were the initials "MB." With the exception of the number "5" added in the middle — these are the same numbers I found in Mr. Rivera's medical chart — in the exact same sequence. What do they mean? According to the medical records I saw with my own eyes, Mark Bringleson never examined or even met Herman Rivera, so how could he be aware of any of those numbers?

The medical records for Anit Chima, Herman Rivera and Danny Garcia are "no longer available." The official story from the hospital board is that Dr. Mark Bringleson suffered a nervous breakdown and moved back to the states.

Eminence, of the five people directly affected by an incident involving an alleged visage of The Holy Mother — one is dead, one is in hiding, and the remaining three are missing! I am no longer a brave man, and therefore, I don't waste paper because I don't like having extra pieces of it hanging about.

I have nothing but my faith to ensure this letter will reach you. This, I swear, is all I know and believe to be true, so help me Almighty God.

"Had it not been for you, I would have never found my way to God."

- Emil D. Azevedo, MD

Father Josef, the elderly priest, who once reluctantly served as the living embodiment of God before a world of hypocritical, unrepentant sinners, gently laid down the pages of Dr. Brigleson's letter. He picked up the news article and glanced at it so furtively, it could have been mistaken for a slow blink. He then closed his eyes and softly whispered a single phrase from the final page of the typed letter from memory, "I don't waste paper."

In one fluid motion, Josef's gnarled fingers scooped up the white envelope that had contained the pages of the letter. He began to carefully peel away at the edges of the envelope and found it had not been manufactured, but rather constructed by hand from a single sheet of paper. In the center of what was once the inside of the "envelope" thirteen numbers were handwritten in pencil, followed by the initials M.B.

−16101456193227−M.B.

Josef scrutinized the digits and ran a forefinger over the lead used to write them. His head slowly leaned to one side as he studied the numbers from a slightly different angle. A slow smirk of understanding began to make its way across his weathered face and a gleam rose in his eyes. He soundlessly leapt from his seat like a man more than half his age, allowing the paper he had been holding to drop, as if forgotten, from his hand onto the floor.

He swiftly traversed the dozen or so steps across the smoothly tiled floor from his sitting nook toward his study, which counted for most of the space in the modest three-room bungalow. Once there, he began to systematically rummage through the pages of the countless books and papers stored on the shelves of his personal library. He had always maintained a veracious passion for reading, especially anything having to do with world studies, geography, history and language. Amongst several other coveted religious scholarly items and artifacts, the four dozen shelves in Josef's study were filled with folders laid neatly atop one another, all containing photographs and religious articles he had clipped himself.

There were three separate sets of Encyclopedia Britannica, countless books and magazines on subjects varying from theological history to philosophy and archeology, to the musings of Khalil Jubran, and the insightful works of Tennessee Williams. The shelves also held many priceless, well-worn, ancient Jewish texts, some of which were still in their centuries-old, original, animal skin bindings. Josef's devotion both to God and the church afforded him access to these and the countless other written treasures held secure within the subterranean vaults of The Vatican.

In his current state of mind, he dreaded to think of what might become of him were he to be set loose amongst those sacred documents now. A part of him wondered if he would perhaps go insane; his conscious brain was unable to handle such a vast flood of information – information he would retain to the minutest detail until the day he died. If someone were to ask him the name of the street he lived on as a child, he wouldn't be able to say. But, without effort, he could easily recall every detail of every single thing he saw, heard and read that night so many years ago, when he tried to outrun the will of God.

Josef's hands trembled as he ran them over and across the many books and papers on the shelves in his library. Only now, they trembled with excitement and in anticipation of the task at hand.

As his fingers caressed the aged leather and paper bindings, or one of the many withered and faded newspapers bundles printed in various languages, Joseph could almost hear a voice inside his head telling him to disregard a book or, conversely, to pull a particular bundle from its well-worn, rubber-band binding.

The first thing Josef retrieved was a yellowed bundle of newspaper clippings. They were so old, the rubber band stretched around them had deteriorated and melded onto itself and the tissue-thin paper. He unrolled the bundle very carefully, as if he expected it to fall apart like some ancient artifact. It took him less than a minute to find what and where to begin his search.

Within the folds of numerous pages of a 1968 Egyptian newspaper called the *Lah varah*, he found the point from which to begin. It was an article detailing the firsthand account of a witness who was part of a mass sighting of the Virgin Mary on April 2, 1968 in El Zeitoun, Cairo. The apparition manifested itself on the rooftop of a church, and according to several witnesses and photographs taken during the event, the Holy Mother was accompanied by seven winged beings.

For over five hours, Father Josef followed a trail of newspaper and magazine articles and cross-referenced them with prophetic writings from antiquity. He read the writings of little-known scholars and long forgotten holy men who had come before him.

He found additional reports of sightings of the Blessed Mother and cross-referenced their geographical locations with world maps and historical events. The old priest poured over antiquated and faded astronomical charts from Tunisia, China and Timbuktu, studying the night skies and the placement of various celestial bodies as they had been thousands of years before Christ walked the earth. Until, at last, he found that which he hadn't realized he was seeking, and the revelation was stunning.

Before long, Josef made his way back to his favorite armchair, his head already beginning to clear from the nameless state of mind he acquired from the drink. The entity within him – along with its insatiable thirst for the written words of men and perhaps knowing its task had been completed – had left the old man. Josef no longer felt its presence, and the alcohol that had brought it about had no lingering effects whatsoever.

He sat in the armchair for over three hours. He didn't remember retrieving the pages of the letter from the floor or folding them neatly before placing them on the little table. No, something else had seen to that. Darkness fell around his little cottage and over the secluded grounds affectionately known as the Gardens of the Vatican. All was quiet with the exception of an occasional breeze rustling through the shrubbery beneath Josef's sitting room window.

The sound of a lone church bell ringing somewhere off in the distance eventually interrupted his indulgence. Those few solitary moments of silent, self-aggrandizement one has when knowing he, and him alone, holds an answer or key to some question or dilemma. At last, having decided the inevitable had been put off long enough, Josef arose from his armchair, with hip joints once again popping and creaking loudly in protest. He stuffed the letter and the piece of paper, which had been used as an envelope, securely into his front pants pocket. And after retrieving a light jacket off a metal hook near the front door and taking his beloved rosary in hand, Father Josef exited the cottage and walked out into the night.

There were very few lights along the garden path on the property, but the old priest had no need of them.

He made his way across the grass and starting walking the pathless route leading up from the quiet gardens and into the private residence of the current head of the Roman Catholic Church. He had taken this route countless times when he himself held the post. How often, he mused, had he trekked through the gardens at night to meditate in solitude? He wondered what they would do, those who were now in power inside the church. Josef thought they were much too often preoccupied with ways in which to retain their power at any cost.

He shook these and other dark musings from his head, his mind briefly grappling with the truth of knowing he would most likely have no say in whatever decisions were made regarding his discovery – a discovery that was simple enough, merely a letter that had been mistaken for a number. Dr. Brigleson's number "5" had actually been the capital letter "S" to delineate a southerly direction. The numbers were, in fact, the exact geographical coordinates for an ancient site in South America, a rock carving in Hayu Marca, Peru known as "The Puerta de Hayu Marca" or "The Gate of the Gods."

Josef increased his gait. Something within him knew there was little time to lose. If the church was indeed investigating the sighting at the statue in Rio, and he harbored little doubt of this not being the case, he would tell them there was nothing more to be gained there. Those who had seen the Holy Mother in Rio had served their purpose. And those who were yet to be touched by, and bear witness to events already set in motion by the hand of The Almighty should go to Hayu Marca. Just as he suspected, Anit Chima, Herman Rivera and Mark Bringleson had been compelled to do. And as he, Father Josef, would now do, with or without the blessing of the church.

17

Yum Dreams of Archs

Yum was aware he was dreaming. Even here, in the depths of his own mind, he found he was weary, but somehow, he knew the burdensome feeling would soon pass, for he sensed the burden he now felt in his spirit was not his own. Here in his dream, he sat comfortably on crimson- colored silk cushions that had been intricately embroidered with delicate strands of gold thread. The effect of this embroidery made the smooth clothe shimmer underneath the gold light of the torches standing upright in the corners of the ethereal room in which he now found himself.

The room was almost uncomfortably spacious. As long as it was wide with high ceilings, it was almost impossible for Yum's mind to fathom. And yet, here he sat alone, cradled by soft cushions and being needled with a mental fatigue he felt quite sure was not of his making. Whatever burden his mind carried, it was not his own. This much he knew. Then, finally, Yum did what he had been created to do – he listened. At first there was only silence, an absence of sound. Then he realized the soft golden light emanating from the torches was created from something man could not yet conceive of.

Yum felt something, although he didn't know what, was about to begin. And so it did – somewhere far above his head, a pure tenor voice broke the silence and filled the expanse of the room.

"Brother, I am awake, hear me." It was the voice of Erik, one of the Keepers who had been transformed, and it was not a question. It was a command. Yum's immediate thought was to reply, but the one to whom the question had been directed responded first:

"Yes, my brother, I, too, have arisen. Are you unwell?" Yum found the voice familiar but could not readily identify who had spoken.

"No, I am well," said Erik. The sound of the tenor in his "new" voice resonated through Yum's spirit and coaxed involuntary tears from his eyes.

"And the body by which you will travel, is it well?" inquired the other with the deeper voice.

"Yes, it ... he, too is quite well. I have wept for him and we have each set aside our fears. How very brave our hosts are and have been." Erik sounded reflective and somewhat saddened by the words he spoke.

At least Yum was fairly sure it was indeed Erik he was hearing; in perhaps the strangest dream he had ever had.

"There is truth in what you say," the other deeper voice responded and continued. "Yet, none of us can truly prepare for the pain and anguish Man has yet to endure."

"If he can, and does indeed, endure," Erik replied.

"Indeed, if he does ... indeed." It was now the deeper toned of the two that sounded reflective.

"We are to depart soon from this, our sanctuary. Are we not, brother?" Erik's voice had changed; it now sounded different somehow.

"Yes. Soon, The Creator shall resound within, and we will take our leave. But for now, repose and rejoice, for although the task is daunting and dark, it is done in reverence to Him and the Earth, which He loves." The deeper toned voice echoed in Yum's mind.

"But what of Man?" asked the voice Yum had supposed was Erik's, but now it seemed to be someone or something else.

"I cannot answer you, brother, for although I inhabit his flesh, I have not the spirit of a Man. Only Man can answer your question. Only Man knows what his kind will become in the presence of his Creator," the deeper toned voice answered.

There was a long, palpable silence following this last statement from the deeper voice, a silence that lasted long enough for Yum to replay in his mind all he had heard. He chastised himself because even as he dreamed, he knew he would be unable to recall every detail of what he had seen and heard upon awakening from the dream, despite all its current detail. He knew this in spite of the fact there was no dream Yum had ever had that he wasn't able to recall in precise detail. And yet, somehow, he knew this particular dream would be the exception. But then there was more, and the deeper voice spoke once again.

"Bezalel, are you still troubled? Are you still there?"

"Yes, Brother Amun, here am I."

"Rest then, rest before our Father calls you to rise up in His name."

"Yes, and may His peace be with you and may the blessing of His hand rest upon your shoulders forever."

"And may the same be with you, my brother ... the same be with you," the deeper toned. Yum sensed perhaps it was the older of the two voices. Yum also sensed that perhaps it had been Terris' and Erik's voices he had been hearing in this dream, and a part of him wondered if he would remember their heavenly names.

And with that, the voices of The Iyrin Amun and Bezalel, and the overwhelming presence Yum had distinctly felt with them, was gone from the room and, subsequently, the recesses of his mind. Yum's body crumpled into the soft cushions upon which his dream-self sat, and he was instantly reunited with his physical self in what soon became a deep and dreamless slumber.

18

The Words of the Creator

I shall remove them from your side. The men of the Earth hath placed their foot upon the necks of their women so much as to stop the flow of life's blood and remove the familiar desire from within her. Woman has not gathered her children unto her bosom and raised them up to My countenance. Low is the counting of the number of issues who know My voice when I walk amongst them. Loud is the wailing of the women of the Earth, as is the bleating of the ewe having lost sight and scent of its master. So preoccupied has the male of the species become with his desire to be Divine, that he has not looked beyond his shoulder to lead or guard those who fill his prints as he treads. Man cannot be without woman, nor woman without man. But, I find neither who have surpassed the mark of thirteen cycles of life worthy of my continued affection.

Therefore, I shall remove all such issue from your sight. For you are no longer worthy to continue. The arrogance of man would have him believe the Beings of Heaven would fling aside the gates and manifest at his side. This is the folly of man's pride. I tell you this – the foundation of the Earth was prepared and set aside for you, my beloved man, yet you would stain it with blood and sin in my name.

I leave you to sort among yourselves who is yet worthy of my favor and the everlasting fruits of the Earth. But I tell you now: it shall be done not upon the backs of or fueled by the blood of the innocent.

All who are of age – fourteen cycles or more–the calculation of which is to include the first full beating of the blood within the womb. All who are of this age and above shall decide the fate of your world. As I am here, so also is evil personified and with many willing hands to lift up its dark purpose. Each man and woman will be measured by his or her merit. Whether ye tread with the Evil One or with the righteous – do so firmly, for the coming days will be long and the waters of the Earth will once again turn red with blood before the day is won or lost. For when next I see you, I will know whether to extend My hand in a peaceful joyous greeting, or to smite Humankind from the Earth and leave the Evil One to his spoils.

Man has greatly altered the world and so therefore, I will alter man in kind. There will be those born and made to see into the hearts of men. They will be made to know My voice and the voices of the Divine. Any who smite them in the name of witchcraft, smite Me also. They shall hear that which you cannot. They shall see that which is hidden from your mortal eyes. But in this, as in all things concerning man – the nature of their character will be the foundation upon which they stand.

Know now ... my vexation with Mankind runs deep. When next I turn My eye to you, know My action will be swift and without language or reason.

For you have known all you need to know to ensure your salvation or your destruction. Those who would kill in My name shall die in My name. Those who would harm the giver of life shall be put to death by Me. The daughters of Eve are mine and her sons are their shepherds. Just as the ewe sustains your life with milk and meat, woman is the vessel by which life is brought forth into the Earth. Defile or bruise woman and the blood of your line shall be henceforth poisoned.

Blessed is he in My eyes who shelters and feeds the widow.

Cursed is he who curses his mother or the mother of his wife, or the mother of his children.

Any man who does such will be reviled by his fellows. Give unto a woman her sons and daughters to raise until the thirteenth annum has passed. This is when a child shall choose his path in life for good or evil. And you will let them go their way from you in peace."

The Iyrin Amun Laments for Mankind

My Father! Oh, my Father – not the children! Do not take their young, for surely they will slaughter themselves. They have not the faith of the men of old, when man was still new, when he knew your voice and the sound of your steps amongst the trees. This age of Mankind – this "new man" lives away from your countenance and seeks not the comfort of your presence. The children they bear are the last vestiges of their faith.

Oh, My Father! If you remove their offspring, I fear all innocence will then truly be wiped from the face of the Earth. It is a sadness that they are no longer worthy of the chance to redeem their souls through the innocent blood of their offspring. Thy will be done, my Father ... you have only to speak it, and Thy Will Be Done.

19

Omael and Amun

"**B**rother, soon the seal will be unbound – is this not so?" These were the thoughts of the Omael, who secretly feared he might never get used to having become one with the confines and unbearable "heaviness" of woman's mortal flesh. Everything about the body he now occupied made him feel as though sacks of sand had been strapped to the legs, arms, head and neck of it. He literally hurt all over and immediately felt deep sorrow for all things mortal upon the Earth.

Omael lay encased in the body of Yukiro, nestled beneath hand-woven linens on a cot the humble and kind Keepers of the temple had afforded he and his brethren so their physical forms might recover from their recent transformation with whatever small comfort the Keepers could muster for them.

He stared inquisitively at the rough-hewn wood ceiling of his darkened chamber and silently directed his thoughts to his brother, The Arch Amun.

"Yes, it is so. When the first of us departs, that which shields this place will be unbound." Amun's reply came as a gentle whisper to Omael's mind.

"Then I shall remain a while with those who are here for it is certain the others will soon find their way to this place," Omael countered.

"It is certain, yes. But this is not your purpose, and your task should take precedence. You do this of your own will, brother?"

"I do," Omael replied quietly.

"And there has been no ... objection?" Amun's tone held the mildest air of surprise.

"None that I have perceived, no." Omael sounded certain.

"Omael, you must honor and retain that body. If you do not, you make little of what has been given."

"There is no one to fight for them. With them. And they, too, have given much. Some, much more than others," Omael insisted.

"The unseen remain among us, Brother," Amun reminded him.

"And without a host, ill-effective, I fear. I will stay and do what I can, what I must. I will not sacrifice this flesh, and I will join you among Man after it is finished." Omael had grown resolute in his decision.

"Omael ..." Amun began.

"Brother, the one who hears listens to us even now, and he is afraid." Omael's reply was thick with empathy.

Amun, who was firmly anchored within the form of the mortal man formerly called Terris Jackson, sighed heavily, as he lay on the narrow cot of in own bedchamber, before replying, "Then he is wiser than most, my brother. He is wiser than most."

Amun let this last thought drift toward the mind of his brother, The Iyrin Omael, before turning over on his side to allow the human body he now inhabited to rest. And while the mortal coil took its rest, Amun allowed his essence to return to that of his father, The Creator, at whose side he found his own much-needed solace and comfort for what would surely be the last time before the Earth shifted and the end of man and his kind began.

20

Yum's Divine Gifts

Before Yum could rap lightly upon the wood door of Terris' room, a voice spoke softly from within.

"Ah, Master Yum." Terris voice was quiet, and knowing.

"Yes, it is I, Divine." Yum spoke tentatively as he entered the room, which was illuminated by only the natural fading sunlight from the unshuttered window. Terris wore a pair of fresh, brown linen pants and a light-colored tunic as he gazed out the small window. It looked to Yum like he was listening to some far-off sound no one but he could hear.

"Please, call me 'Terris'. This is the name given this man, and we honor him in keeping it, for he is not apart from me." Terris turned and greeted Yum with a wide, welcoming smile.

"As you say, Terris," Yum replied, feeling terribly uncomfortable. "I have done as I was instructed. It came to me in a dream. I only hope the work is to your liking."

Yum reached into the small sachet tied at his waist and carefully extracted and surrendered an amulet constructed with a dark blue iridescent and shiny stone at its center. The stone was intricately wrapped with thin strands of braided hemp that culminated into two thicker strands. "I have made each so they can be tied onto whatever you wish," Yum offered humbly.

"It is wondrous. I shall wear mine around my neck."

To Yum's horrified surprise, Terris lowered his head so the elder man could place the amulet around his neck. Yum secured the amulet at the nape of Terris' neck, while silently praying over the final knot. His prayer was that the knot would remain in place until the man or Being bowed before him meets his Father in Heaven, yet again.

"Thank you, Master Yum," Terris said with genuine gratitude and again, in an all-knowing tone. He stood upright, which left Yum with little doubt The Iyrin had "heard" his prayer.

"Go now and give the others theirs. Soon my companions and I will be directed to leave this sacred place. You were entrusted with the elements expelled during our transformation into flesh, and you have turned that which was foul into objects worthy of Heaven. You have done well, for through these, we will be reminded of the sacrifice of man's flesh for The Creator's purpose. These will serve to stay our hand against Our Father's most beloved in the darkness that is to come. For it is not the place of The Iyrin to judge man nor to strike them down for their great sins against God or His daughter, Earth," Terris sighed wearily and turned his back to the window before continuing.

"But whatever do you mean? It is written in every religion on Earth that God will see to the judgment of man. Isn't this why you have come? To usher in God's time of judgment?" Yum sounded frightened, and small again like a child.

Terris did not move from where he stood but kept his back to Yum when he spoke, and his voice was a sorrowful whisper. "No, Master Yum. You shall judge yourselves. And all of Heaven weeps for you."

Yum said nothing, he simply didn't understand what the unearthly being meant by the statement, and a part of him didn't wish to know. As if reading his thoughts, Terris spoke again, this time with a slightly more authoritative tone.

"It is a complicated thing to understand, but no matter. You have done well. Go swiftly now, and give to my companions what belongs to them. The time of our sanctuary draws to an end."

Terris' eyes flicked abruptly toward the Western view of the Celestial Mountains and his brow furrows became hard and stern. He was once again listening to something Yum was certain no mortal ear was capable of hearing. A look of disdain briefly crossed the erstwhile serene face of the Divine and, in that moment, Yum was quite content and grateful to be merely a mortal man. For he had suddenly come to understand that somewhere, somehow, something had been wise to insist mortal man need not know all the secrets in the universe.

The brief encounter with the look of deep concern moving over a Divine being's face had caused his flesh to crawl with an unfettered sense of dread. If a Divine creature such as this were moved to this level of concern over a thing as yet unseen, then surely the origins of what was unseen could not be of the world in which a man lived, and it was, therefore, never meant to be seen by mortal eyes.

The Tyrin Speak

"Learning to Live"

Learning how to live is not always a process that is without pain

Pain is essential

It is there to help us remember our errors

The greater the pain the better the lesson learned

Know that in time you will be capable of seeing a lesson at its end

Remember that as with any favorite subject

There are some that we do not wish to end

Learn to let go

For if you have retained the beginning

You will return to the subject with the eagerness and ease of the Master

21

A Battlement of Stones

Amun felt the embodiment of the evil ones long before he heard them toiling, scratching, and crawling and at times, slipping and falling throughout the crevasses and valleys of the mountains. Corrupted and tormented, they made their impossible way toward the hidden gates of The Keep like a wild horde of black winged hornets the size of men with the scent of fresh blood burning in their nostrils. Little was it known by those within the walls of the temple that these soulless human bodies, overshadowed and animated by evil, would be every bit as ruthless, but with more than one stinger to give for their wasted flesh because the life force of The Creator no longer dwelled within them.

The human bodies fast approaching the temple had answered a call, as well, that of those who served the first and who fell in defiance of God. And like those who had waited so long in these mountains, they had also waited in some similar but perhaps darker place on Earth.

Yes, Amun heard their impending approach, even as they emerged from the darkest corners of the Earth. They were every bit as resolute to reach The Keep as those who had built its walls, intending them to protect the souls within.

The hearts of those who were coming were filled with the black pitch of hate, just as much as The Keeper's hearts were filled with the patience of servitude and the purity of love.

Both compelled by that which willed them to find this sacred place, each for the same reason: to usher in the time of the judgment of Mankind, albeit in two different ways. The struggle for Earth and the favor of God had begun.

Yes, Amun had heard evil begin its inevitable ascent through the mountains yet remained silent. He said nothing, as he and the other Iyrin, each within the privacy of their rooms, simultaneously began to quietly pack weathered goatskin knapsacks with the meager provisions required to sustain their human forms. The eleven of them then met in silence in the outer courtyard of the temple.

Erik, who carried a large wooden staff in one hand and his knapsack over his shoulder, grinned eagerly at everyone and to no one in particular. Paolo, Gunaar, Shylo, Elishiva, Yukiro, Milos and the Moshi twins remained stoic in their demeanor. Randle, who stood closest to Erik and was about three feet shorter, nudged the larger man gently and smiled. All had chosen to wear the amulets given them by Yum around their necks, with the exception of Yukiro, who wore hers around her wrists.

The stones glowed like brightly colored beacons as they stood together in the darkness. Amun shed the body of Terris and stood before his brethren as Iyrin when he spoke:

"Go before man and watch as Our Father bids. Answer to the name of the flesh you inhabit, remember your purpose is unto God, not Man. Heed the will of Our Father until he calls you home."

He then turned and spoke to the Moshi twins:

"Sepheriel, Sandelphon, your time is here. May Our Father's mercy be upon Mankind in this dark hour. Go!"

With this, the twins were transformed into two bright pillars of light that flashed upward and streaked across the night sky like two meteors. There was another flash of light, and in an instant, Terris was once again standing among the others in the courtyard.

"Then it has truly begun," Elishiva's voice was resolute and ready.

"Yes, and I shall see you again in Heaven when it is done," Terris replied with a smile. Elishiva turned and walked off into the darkness leaving no footprints as she passed, and within moments she was gone.

"I go to Pakistan," Randle said matter-of-factly before turning and walking down one of the darkened temple corridors.

Shortly thereafter and without saying a word, Shylo the African, Gunaar the German, and Milos turned and exited the courtyard at the same time and were gone.

"Well, they could have said something." Erik said, sounding a little hurt as he sat crossed-legged on the ground, placing both his staff and backpack down at his side.

"We were not meant to know. Your directive will come, be patient," said Yukiro.

"Omael is right, it will come. And you more than any of us will know more than all of us combined – for this is your purpose," Terris offered.

"Amun, didn't you just tell us we were to answer to the names of our hosts? My name is Erik." He offered a toothy grin as he teased Terris.

"My apologies, Erik." Terris grinned and bowed deeply toward Erik, who smiled before suddenly becoming very serious and jumping to his feet. Yukiro and Terris remained still, as Erik started behaving as though he can hear something they cannot. Erik gathered up his belongings and turned toward the darkened corridor inside the temple, from which the others exited to get to the courtyard.

Before anyone could speak, Yum appeared in the courtyard's alcove. He is dressed for travel and has a small packed knapsack and a blanket rolled up and strapped to his back.

Yukiro stepped forward and was about to speak, when Terris raised a hand and shook his head at her.

"I was told to pack a bag and meet you here." Yum searched each of their faces before his gaze settled on Erik.

"Then, come." Erik spoke as though he was trying to coax a lamb.

"But I am too old to leave," Yum said. His voice was barely a whisper and he seemed to be filled with shame.

"Evil is coming to this place." Erik's focus was completely on Yum, and his voice was soothing, patient, and gentle.

"I know. I can hear them. But I cannot make it down the mountains, and I would only slow you down, Divine. I only came because I was told to by something ... someone, a voice greater than I have ever heard before." Tears streamed down the old man's face as he sputtered out his last words. It was clear he had been trying to be obedient in packing his few belongings before humbly presenting himself to these heavenly hosts in the temple courtyard in the middle of the night.

Yum's humility brought tears to Erik's eyes, and he wiped them away with the back of his hand before allowing his staff to fall to the ground. He stepped forward to embrace the weeping old man.

Terris and Yukiro looked on in silence, as Erik – a scholarly giant of a man – bent on one knee to embrace and comfort Yum as though he were a frightened child.

After a moment, Erik looked toward the sky and in response, what clouds there were in the night sky parted and the courtyard brightened with moonlight.

"Master Yum, look down at the ground and tell me what you see," said Erik, as he stood back up, still grasping the old man's shoulders.

Yum looked down toward the ground and there in the moonlight he saw the shadows both he and Erik cast upon the ground. Then, the old man's eyes went wide and his mouth fell open as he bore witness to the shadows of not one but *three* massive and emensly powerful looking wings as their shadows expanded from the right side of Erik's sillouette with such silent purity and grace, it was only by God's hidden hand Yum's soul did not seek it's maker then and there. The largest wing looked to be at least ten feet long and extended from the upper shoulder area, while the second wing, which was only slightly smaller than the first, extended from below the larger wing at Erik's waist. The shadow of the smallest apendage, which appeared to be at least as long as Yum was tall, was attached at the point just below the base of Erik's calf. Only the shadow of the largest wing was fully extended, and Yum guessed the smallest of the three which had remained almost completely folded in half, would easily measure four and a half feet long!

When Yum's breath sucked in and his body went stiff, the shadow of the larger wing bent back and forth as if it were waving at him. Yum smiled involuntarily and Erik let out a hearty laugh.

"You shall travel in the shadow of that wing my friend. My Father bid me keep you by my side and this I will do." The levity was gone from Erik's voice.

"But how am I ...?" Yum began.

"No! Do not ask how you shall keep up – just know I will keep you. All you need do is have faith and remain in the shadow of my wing, yes?" Erik made this last request with a small encouraging smile.

"Yes, Divine." Yum's confidence returned and the moonlight faded from the courtyard once again.

"And it's Erik ... not 'Divine'," Erik said, retrieving his staff. "Come, we'd better get started." Erik and Yum began to make their way toward the entryway through which Yum had entered the courtyard, when Erik stopped to look back at Terris and Yukiro.

"Until we return home, brothers!" Erik said, raising his staff and smiling broadly. Erik's gaze lingered on Terris, and the two exchanged a brief nod, as The Iyrin within each acknowledge the thanks one had given the other for saving his life and nursing him back to health. When the moment had passed, Erik continued down the passageway with Yum on his left side, and he swiftly moved the older man to the right side of his body before they disappeared into the darkness of the hallway.

"Do not ask how – just know that I will." Yukiro repeated Erik's words. "If only the first of them could have understood this," she reflected, while looking at the empty doorway through which Erik and Yum had just retreated.

She and Terris remained silent for several moments before she abruptly transformed into a pillar of light, and, in a flash, disappeared back inside the temple, leaving her packed belongings behind.

After Yakiro had gone, Amun was alone in the courtyard, encased within the body of Terris Jackson, never once having the impulse to question the whereabouts or the tasks given his departed brethren. His thoughts were connected to those of The Creator and the sound of the more than a thousand deranged humans who were making their way through the mountains toward The Keep with the sole intent of obliterating it and all within, from and off the face of the Earth.

And yet, The Iyrin were not the only ones moved to rise long before the sun to prepare for what was coming to the gates of Temple Khan Tengre. As the sun rose over The Celestial Mountains of the Tian Shan and shone its golden light perhaps for the last time upon the entrance of the sacred Keep, The Stones stood firmly in place. They were a human interlocking net of bone, sinew, muscle and skin, woven in an ancient acrobatic feat of flexibility, the sight of which went beyond human understanding and description.

Firmly clasped hands to forearms and legs, they stood, some with their ancient bodies contorted in positions seemingly unnatural to the human form. Some were bent into complete hyper-extended backbends as they stood on the shoulders of others. Along the edges of the stone floor and walls, they bent and clasped their hands underneath the ridges of stone lining the building to protect and offer a barrier between the good residing behind the gateway of The Keep and the evil that was to ascend from below.

Near the base of this gate of flesh, stood an elderly black woman whose name the mortal man Terris had never known. A woman who had brought the newly arrived Iyrin, Amun, fresh linens once, a woman whose soul Amun knew completely. Her name was Phyllis, and she was standing on the shoulders of a frail looking Chinese woman, whose age on any given day would have been guessed to be no less than 108.

Phyllis' womanly frame stood firmly, solid as rock with her head turned, strained but firm over her right shoulder. She stood atop the Chinese woman's shoulders with her toes curled so tightly they dug into the fabric of the older woman's tunic and most likely her flesh, as well. It was a death grip, in more ways than one.

Amun remembered the afternoon she tried to joke with him about her bold escape from a hospital in Arizona. How she had wandered off the grounds in the middle of the day at the age of 89, leaving her hometown to come across the planet to this place. Amun had laughed then, even as she went on to tell him about her granddaughter, who she guessed would be nearly fifty-two years old.

Phyllis knew in her heart she probably had several great-grandchildren she would never meet, not in this life, anyway. Yes, Amun had laughed then, but he was not laughing now.

She looked at him with both pity and affection, and before her eyes glazed over white and went completely blank, Amun allowed her to see his true countenance, wings and all. She smiled sweetly before retreating into the center place in her mind that only she and The Creator knew, the place where there would be no more pain and where the labor of breathing would soon end. Where she would fully and freely retreat and will her body to become stone, and the place where she would allow her purpose on this Earth to be fulfilled.

He watched in silence at the last of them, an elderly bald Caucasian man, who Amun saw in his mind's eye holding a broom, and Amun knew it was Terris who was remembering the man. He continued to watch in silence as the man nimbly climbed up onto the shoulders of an even older man, locking limbs with him before turning into stone right before his eyes. Amun understood then that Phyllis had told him the truth: she had gifted a part of her life to him, perhaps because only he, as Terris, having been the one who had most recently come from the world she had known, would understand. He would remember Phyllis.

Amun would remember her and a doctor with the surname of "Who," a man with curly hair she and her granddaughter liked to watch on television together in the afternoon after the granddaughter came home from school.

Yes, he would remember the Old Stones who were, even now, gracefully and some perhaps gratefully, giving up their lives to allow he and the other Iyrin and the goodly Yum time to make their way down the mountain and escape. A tear of pity escaped Amun and ran down Terris' cheek, and in the tear was perhaps the last remnant of Terris Jackson's humanity. Amun turned away from The Stones of The Gardens at Temple Khan Tengre, and away from Phyllis' vacant gaze and her serene, frozen smile. For the hoards had reached the base of the valley and people could be heard yelling and crashing their way through the forest in the foothills below, and also in the cliffs above the temple. Many were screaming incoherent madness and there were dogs among them, for there was wild barking and howling.

Inside the temple the remaining Keepers did what they could to secure the inner walls of the temple. But in truth, there was not much they could do; the temple had been built as a place of peace and waiting, not of battle. In his wisdom, Shihan had gathered the one hundred or so souls who remained in the center of The Keep, making certain to pair a younger Keeper with an older one for comfort's sake. When the screaming hoard reached the outer edges of the temple and a rock was thrown through one of the open windows, Shihan stood upon a reading table.

"Look to me and remember the voice that called you here." He spoke as though there was nothing but a quiet breeze outside and all could hear him.

Li, the physician, had been given the task of looking into all the rooms to make sure everyone had gathered to Shihan's side. But afterwards – despite his fear and the deafening sounds made by the insane, who were throwing rocks and tearing at the walls of the temple – he ran toward the outer courtyard. He found Terris standing inside the barrier created by the human stones, untouched and unmoved by the melee around him. On the other side of the barrier, he saw faces twisted by hate and insanity, evil, filth-stained things with eyes devoid of life or hope. They hissed and bled, some were even unclothed with skin badly damaged by the elements and the violent trek up the mountain from God only knows where.

In his mind, Li thought, *If one of these people, these things, were to strike a flare or light a fire to the temple, they would be doomed and burned alive.* He frantically ran up to the body housing The Iyrin Amun and pleaded, "Don't you see what's happening? Can't you do something? Help us! Help us fight!" His eyes were filled with tears as the hoards directed by the evil one began to slash and tear at what had become the slick, marble-like flesh of The Stones. Although the flesh had become firm, still the blood flowed, which made their task more difficult. The surface of the stones of the garden had become slick and sticky with torn flesh and blood, but their grip upon one another held fast.

"Oh. My. God." Li's eyes went wide with shock and he slowly backed away one slow step at a time until he tripped and fell over backwards.

"Come, it is time." It was Yukiro. She had emerged from the doorway behind the terrified doctor, and Li screamed in fright at the sound of her voice. With one swift movement, she effortlessly lifted him to his feet and ushered him back inside the temple. Terris gathered both his backpack and Yukiro's and swiftly followed them. By the time Yukiro reached the spot where Shihan and the others had gathered, she was carrying Li underneath one arm. The whole of the space stood empty now, but rocks and debris were landing with regularity.

The sound of everything within the temple being destroyed, crashing and breaking against the walls or on the ground could be heard echoing throughout the halls. At one point, a terrible thudding sound made the walls shudder. Yukiro moved swiftly through the halls and deeper into the bowels of the temple, until she finally stepped down a few stone steps and stopped at the doors Shihan had, at one time, believed he had sealed forever. Except now the doors were wide open and beyond them, surrounded on the floor by the remnants of the ancient seal, stood Shihan and his faithful Keepers. Yukiro had opened the doors that Shihan thought to shut forever. And it was here, just outside the chamber, where The Iyrin had arrived and she had brought him and the others to keep them safe.

Terris turned around and closed the two outer doors behind him, an action that immediately cut off the sounds of mayhem taking place throughout the Temple. He turned and faced Shihan, who was standing with his back against the doors.

"Is this where we are to meet our end?" Shihan asked Terris directly and without fear. Terris' brown eyes glowed brightly in response; it was a rich and terrible sight. Several of The Keepers retreated in fear and many looked away and began to pray.

"This, His Most Faithful One, is where you go forth." It was Yukiro who replied. Shihan and the others turned to find Yukiro standing near the open doors of the chamber from which they all witnessed The Iyrin emerge.

The doors had been restored and, on either side, floating approximately three feet off the ground was a six-foot pillar of blue light.

"The twelfth and thirteenth pillars," Shihan whispered aloud.

"There is little time. You must go, please." Terris' voice is almost pleading with those he senses are doubting.

"Once inside, you will be kept safe." Yukiro never took her gaze from Shihan.

"Master, no! We cannot!" one of the Keepers cried out.

"I can, and we will. For it is His will." Shihan's reply was simple, calm and final. He smiled broadly, turned, and made his way toward the darkened doorway of the chamber. As he did so, the two pillars standing on either side of the doorway glowed brightly at his approach.

"Thank you, my eyes aren't what they used to be," he chimed cheerfully.

The old master was followed closely and quietly by the other Keepers, and they entered the chamber in groups of three and four all huddled together. The last to enter the chamber was Li, who had not left Yukiro's side.

"Will we die?" Li asked her tentatively, mesmerized by the glowing pillars of light and the darkness beyond.

"Iyrin do not know what it means to die," Yukiro answered him, placing a hand on his shoulder. "But Yomael and Sitael will walk with you if you like."

Li looked at her with tears of gratitude streaming down his face and nodded his head, saying, "Yes. Yes, I would like it very much, thank you." Li then turned to Terris and nodded his head in thanks, and Terris smiled at him warmly.

Yukiro took Li by the shoulders and placed him in the center of the doorway, directly between the two ice-blue pillars of light.

Li looked up at the pillars in awe as they moved closer to him and flanked him on either side.

"So beautiful," Li muttered.

The pillars of light glowed brighter until Li could no longer be seen, and Yukiro stepped back as the light, which had become one massive blue pillar, moved forward into the darkened chamber. The moment the light entered the chamber, the massive doors slammed shut with an earth-shattering boom that shook the very foundation of the temple and the ground upon which Yukiro and Terris stood.

A cracking of the Earth was heard and the doors quaked, shuddered and turned a molten red as they are sealed shut from within. When it was all over, all that remained was a natural rock face with an ugly jagged scar a meter wide.

The scar remains an anomalous vein of molten iron that almost looks as though it was made from a mighty blow of an angel's sword.

By mid-morning on April 28, 2027, Terris and Yukiro were at the base of the Celestial Mountains watching thick black plumes of smoke rising and billowing over the white snow-caps. The only lives lost that morning would be those of the poor souls the Evil One had left to freeze to death in the mountains. Those souls had been given over to him long before they were called to destroy a little-known temple in the mountains of China.

The two Iyrin walked together for a while, and yet they could not lament those lost, nor question the fates of Shihan or the others they had ushered into the darkened chamber. For this was not their purpose – that task belonged to Cafziel, who now walked the Earth as "Milos." And so, they walked on for a time together in silence until Terris looked up and realized Yukiro was no longer at his side. He did not stop. He did not question. He merely continued onward, waiting contentedly for His Father in Heaven to call on him.

22

The Angry Soldier

After the loss of their child, Maia Joy, Matthew remained with Monica, the woman he had never known how to love, for as long as she had let him try. But soon the madness seething in the minds and hearts of the parents of the world found its way to her, as well. He couldn't save her from it because he was too busy desperately fighting to preserve what was left of his own sanity. And fight he did. He fought the grief and the fear, the terrible silence and the horror of it all. And he came to discover the easiest way for a person to go insane was to try and process how every child on the planet under the age of thirteen had simply ceased to be as easily as his Maia Joy had.

One could not safely attempt to comprehend the utter maniacal, wailing madness that had seized the parents of the world, parents of all ages, races, sex, classes and creeds – God had not given a damn – He took them all! And upon the crest of the wave of the world's insanity came "The Veiled Seas." This phenomenon happened in every country around the world where women had been oppressed, treated as second-class citizens or worse. In the space of forty days, every woman, of every age, creed and color in these counties stopped whatever they were doing and made their way to the largest body of water they could find and calmly walked into it! As the days progressed, they began to walk in herds by the thousands.

At one point, over a hundred thousand women were esti-
mated to be walking across the Jordanian desert, all heading
toward the Red Sea. Their multicolored saris could be seen by
satellite undulating like a living rainbow under the blinding
light of the desert sun. To the best of anyone's knowledge, every
single one of the women made it across the desert alive. They
walked silently and undeterred as if caught in a blissful dream.

Once they reached the sea, their men: sons, fathers, brothers
and husbands, shouted and pulled, hit, cut and even killed some
in an effort to stop the progression. But the women would not
stop; they did not stop. They trampled the men beneath their
feet, they clawed at the men and beat them from them, they fell
and died in the streets from militia gunfire, from knife wounds,
and in some cases, the stones were thrown at their heads – but
the women, in a silent dusty wave of color, flowed over the men.

Some women died on their bellies as they crawled on their
hands and knees toward the wet shores and cliffs of the water
where the tyrant God had called them to die. But it wasn't the
mass suicide that had broken Monica's mind. It was when the
thousands of men to whom these women were bound in one
fashion or another had waded into the seas to retrieve the bodies
of their women. One only had to watch in horror as the countless colored veils, saris, burkas and other nameless innumerable garments and pieces of cloth, which they had demanded
the women conceal themselves with, rose to the surface of the
water devoid of the bodies upon which they had been worn.
There were no bodies. Not one. All that remained were countless swaths of colored cloth floating on the open seas.

Thus, the body of water had been rechristened the "Veiled
Seas," and each man in his own time had gone to retrieve an
armful of fabric and carry the soggy load from the water back
up onto the shore. Once there, the men hung the countless
pieces of colored cloth from the branches of the trees, shrubs
and bushes lining the shores and those further up on the hill-
sides of the land. Then, and to this day three years later, the

faded wispy peach, black, red, white, teal, blue and countless other colors of man and his manufactured world waved and reached out toward the seas like long fingers, as if beckoning their owners to return and willingly bow their heads to once again expose their necks in order to wear the yoke of mortal men. But no more.

Monica remained stone-faced and silent before the television set, after the loss of Maia Joy. Her body and mind spent with grief and worry over her child and perhaps, the world.

Matthew placed a gentle hand on her head and silently stroked her hair in a gesture that was more out of simple human kindness than the love he felt for her. She had not moved, and he didn't say anything.

There was nothing left for them to say to each other. She remained silent, stiff and unmoving underneath his touch, as she had for the past two months. He suddenly felt dirty for touching her, and he retreated to the bathroom so the shower he didn't need could mask the sound of his own terrible sobs. When he came out of the bathroom some thirty minutes later, the house was dark and quiet as the tomb it had become. Monica was gone.

She was gone, and he let her go. At the time and now, three years later, he could not think of one good reason to bring her back. They both knew there was nothing for them to come back to or for. He stayed alone in the house for weeks, no more concerned or preoccupied by her absence than he had been when she left.

One night, he stood in the darkened narrow hallway of the house. All the lights were out, and he was fairly sure the man standing across the street underneath the murky yellow glow of the streetlight couldn't see a thing through the bay window from which he was being observed by Matthew. And yet the man stood with his hands shoved deep inside his pockets and stared directly into Matthew's face as if they were only a few feet apart.

But they were at least a half a football field apart and by all rights, Matthew should have been undetectable standing in a dark house in a narrow hallway. A deeply rooted instinct for survival told him this wasn't true, however. Matthew thought he could feel the man's eyes scrutinizing his face. He tried remembering a time when the stranger had not been there, standing on the sidewalk staring at the house, his gaze penetrating the distance, the glass of the bay window and the darkness within until his gaze found its quarry.

"Quarry." The word jostled something in his mind, but he was too busy looking at the stranger to think just what it was exactly.

Matthew shifted his weight to feel the reassuring presence of the fully loaded Ruger pistol he had strapped low on his hip. He was not sure when he started wearing the gun, but even before witnessing The Event firsthand, he had a nasty feeling the world would quickly be heading toward hell in a hand basket. A .BIG. FAT. ONE. And things did get very dodgy, awful and downright scary as hell!

First, there were the four nearly obliterating rounds of the same deadly pandemic. A virus so rampant and highly contagious, it literally stopped the entire world from functioning for thirty-six months!

And do not forget the voice of God thing that happened, Matthew reminded himself. *You do remember when every single person on the planet heard the voice of the living God in their heads at the same time, don't-cha'? Uh ... yeah ... that. Not now, Matty, gotta keep your wits right now ... don't think about that one just yet, stay with me ... atta boy.*

The viruses were followed by countless people taking their own lives after descending into the madness brought on by grief from the sudden and supernatural taking of their children and the sheer terror of whatever else was still to come. As for

Matthew and those who remained, sane or otherwise - there
was little else left to fear.

Not everything happened exactly how the last few hundred
years of religious speculation and Hollywood movies depicted
it would. The dead hadn't risen from their graves. The mil-
lions who died and could be buried, were buried. And as far as
anyone knew, they stayed that way. Those who managed to survive, albeit barely, and had retained their sanity, still remained
very much above ground.

But eventually, the number of dead surpassed the number of
living who were still mentally and physically capable of properly disposing of potentially infectious remains. Facilitating the
disposal of well over sixty-five million corpses in a sanitary
and relatively timely manner turned out to be a problem of a different sort. As both the labor force and the country's land space
had been virtually depleted in one way or another by death.

Before long, it became necessary for the deceased to be
transported en mass via the railways in hermetically sealed
freight containers. It was rumored these freight trains sometimes stretched on for more than a mile in length. However, it
was also a fact the trains were rarely ever seen running during
daylight hours, because they mostly moved across the country
after the nation was well into the national nightly curfew hours.

But once these metal monstrosities with bellies full of their
morbid cargo started, they absolutely would not stop running
for man, machine nor beast – not until they had delivered the
country's beloved (and still infectious) cargo to a station near
one of the many abandoned rock quarries scattered throughout
parts of the Midwest.

Massive trucks picked up the remains of countless mothers,
fathers, sons, daughters and whatever else they once were to
each other by proxy, and dumped them unceremoniously into
the nearest quarry. A representative from each of the major religious groups stood encased in a glass booth wearing a facemask
while viewing the disposal.

The booth would be lifted above the quarry by a crane and once there, officiates would perform whatever rites were proper and fit for their brand of belief, be they Muslim, Jewish, Christian, Hindu or Buddhist, after which the bodies below were set alight and burned. All religions were welcome to allot a representative to participate ... if they could stomach the stench. It was said you only had to be unfortunate enough to see the hellish glow from one of the quarry fires burning at night once, and it would be more than enough to keep you from sleeping soundly for more than a week. And God forbid you were ever caught downwind of the putrid stink coming from the general direction of one of the fires.

If this were to happen, you might as well burn whatever clothing you were wearing, because the smell would never completely wash out. Interestingly enough, not one religious group ever protested the practice of the mass burnings, and not one atheist ever spoke up.

The Evangelicals had refused to participate altogether, which was just as well, seeing as how they still owned the majority of the satellite and broadcasting companies. They held daily two-hour religious services instead for everyone alive, dying or dead, every day, on every radio and TV channel, whether you wanted to hear it or not.

Of course, there was a buy-out plan, one where you paid an exorbitant fee so you wouldn't have to listen to the daily sermon. Funny, with the Evangelicals there was always a buy-out plan. Matthew wondered if there would be a buy-out plan when the tyrant god pulled his next rabbit out of the hat. Come to think of it, he couldn't remember the last time he had heard from the Evangelicals. Since his Maia and all the other children of the world disappeared, Evangelicals had all but disappeared, too. He guessed they were probably all still on their knees at the negotiation table on that one.

A sound escaped from Matthew's throat, as though he had intended to chuckle at something his heart and mind knew was not the least bit funny. Matthew had come to know the nature of people. It wasn't the facts of a situation that broke a man's mind and spirit; it was the unknown that drove you mad. And what better way for a bully God to test a man's faith than to not say a single solitary word to him ... ever.

Once a man has reached the point of self-annihilation, why not step in and make it so all but the foolish would question your existence? Do this boldly, brazenly and as always, in silence. Strip him of his family, his hearth and home, and keep him out in the cold. And then let him wonder.

Let him guess at his great sin and agonize over the fate of his immortal soul. It did not take long for the streets and cities to fill with men and women driven insane with such speculations.

They were dazed and in denial, still clinging to any pitiful semblance of hope for salvation and forgiveness. They were not often violent, but as violent as any animal desperate for a scrap of food or succor from their suffocating grief. The worst that could be done these days was looking a bereaved crazed mother in the eye and telling her you knew nothing about her missing child. He had once seen a woman scratch her own eyes out while screaming she could look for her missing son no more.

For Matthew, it was the pregnant ones who were the worst. Those bellies, still swollen and stretched taut by the ghosts of developing children, were now inexplicably empty and barren with no trace of water, waste or flesh. The babies they once harbored had simply ceased to be.

And the sight of the haunting, tortured, and dark circled eyes of an expectant mother, whose belly had yet to recede, frightened him more than any Hollywood zombie ever could. Most of those women had either killed themselves or cut themselves open and bled out from the wound long before their bellies had the chance to flatten again.

Something inside of Matthew shifted restlessly, and he instinctively knew the man could see him. He knew that despite the darkness and the distance, the man could see him as plainly as if he were standing no more than an arm's length away in broad daylight.

An uneasy grimace broke across Matthew's face. As if on cue, the man displayed his own toothy grin in response and nodded at Matthew as though pleased he had finally figured out the puzzle. A cold chill ran down the back of Matthew's legs, and he was no longer amused. He realized the cat and mouse game he thought he had been playing was in dire need of some clarification as to which of them was the mouse, and which was the cat. Matthew fingered the handle of the pistol stuffed in the top of his pants just to the right of his spine. He watched the stranger's gaze shift downward, and he knew the man had seen him touch the gun. The man looked right into Matthew's face again, smiled slowly, nodded, and then turned and walked away. Matthew made a mental note, that if he were to run into the sly-smiling son-of-a-bitch again, he'd know exactly which one of them was the cat.

He waited another twenty minutes and then packed a duffle bag along with the photo of Monica and Maia, and left the house without closing the front door behind him, or even bothering to look back. There was no need.

He knew he would not be coming back. Matthew Knightly hated God, and he didn't give a fuck what anyone else had to say about it. He was going to find the deity and kick him squarely in the throat. After that? Well, he figured by then he would most likely be dead - and that was perfectly fine with him.

The Iyrin Prophecy

The Iyrin were sent to all corners of the Earth, separate but connected. Linked only by the knowledge of their bound purpose to The Creator, that of shielding what was left of Humankind from madness upon witnessing the movements of God. The one who first fell will coerce many to his bosom. Those worthy of surviving will be greatly outnumbered, for the dead in spirit have already begun to walk among the living. They will kill and wait to be killed in turn by the hand of an innocent, thus they succeed in murdering yet another soul alongside their own.

Man, in his infancy and humility, was closer to The Creator. But this "new" man – this arrogant thing that dares to stand upright and turn his face toward the heavens in challenge to The Creator and its misguided quest to believe himself on equal ground with that which is Divine is both his folly and his misfortune. Knowledge was the first sin of Man. For all that is does not need to be known to all that exists. Once seen, there are things a Being can no longer deny. How much better is it to be a lamb in the field, than to be an object of sacrifice for one who endlessly spills blood in the name of one whom they shall never appease or even hope to understand, let alone call "equal?"

Humankind, in his arrogance and determination to believe himself "set apart" with a purpose, failed to see how much like his God he was.

For my Father feels pain, anger, glory, love, sorrow, and pride – all of which is poorly reflected in the actions of man. The heavens have oft rocked with the wailings of the Lord until He seldom could turn His loving eye toward the Earth. We cannot save all the sons and daughters of man. Yea, I cannot refrain from destroying them – for surely, they will rise and devour themselves yet again and the Earth along with them.

But in truth, I tell all that is: if the Earth but raise her sweet tones in agony to Mine spirit, I shall come to her swiftly and with little mercy for that which I have belabored her.

Like an Iyrin with a blight upon her countenance, she hath borne the burden that is Man and his fodder upon her. Everything pure and perfect upon and about her has been altered by his presence and his desire to become God. I do not begrudge what I have brought into being, but he has surely been pushed and molded by he who first left Me to mock the heavens through the countenance of Man.

I believed and pitied Man's desire to lease the bosom of Earth in his quest for Me, but this desire is no longer true, and I find it abhorrent that any being would demise all that exists for the sake of his existence. The Divine are not men, and man is not yet Divine.

He who first fell will toy with them until no upright walking flesh lives. Man will wither and die like a spent vine. The fallen one will move on and conquer other gardens. He will leave the Earth quiet and barren, void of all but that which crawls, slinks and scratches upon on all fours.

In time, she will once again become the paradise I and My children intended. But her fury will not suffer any that walk upright again. She would smite them from her as lightening smites the ground. And this I must let be if it shall inflict Mankind upon her, my sweet daughter earth, again.

The Creator will take the children of Man, all those who had not yet reached the age of thirteen years. A day will come when they will turn and thus be gone as if they had calmly walked through an unseen door. And Mankind will rage and turn upon one other, each placing the blame on all and any, save the reflections they encountered each day.

The cries to Heaven will be constant and deafening as Man wails for the return of that which they no longer deserve. The Creator will release the spirits of those whom men have confined. Wombs will fall as the fruits from within wither and die on their vines. And still, Man will rage and weep for his kind.

For a moment, and it was the briefest of time, I was one with The Creator. I was allowed to feel the agony that was the separation of Humankind. Throughout Man's existence, the creatures have sought separation from their source. How alike Mankind is to his inceptor. Man sought his autonomy, and does not Man's offspring strive for autonomy from his begetters? Does not Mankind seek to stand on equal ground with his creator? And does not Man then seek to surpass his creator so that soon he will have no need for that which spoke him into being?

In his arrogance, Man no longer speaks of that which preceded him. Man, from his inception, sought to separate, nay – liberate himself and thus his offspring from the source of his being. Man solved all his own problems, save one – himself. He soon became as arrogant as the fallen one for a time, displaying false repentance until even this simple gesture was lost to Humankind. The arrogance of Man, having seduced himself into believing it was he who had willed himself up from out of the dry and lifeless dust and into being.

For this reason, The Creator has become angered. He gave men His love and the Earth to steward, and protected Humankind from the races of time and space, and from the visions and presence of those Beings that Humankind was still too young to comprehend.

But Man served to please himself and invoked the endless mercy of God in ways he saw fit, until at last, they caused The Creator's precious sphere to cry out in pain and want of relief. This, The Almighty could not bear nor justify.

And, following the third sickness, every mind of Man upon the Earth heard the Lord when He spoke and said unto them: "I will remove all things desired by the hearts of Men in the same manner he denies a petulant child. This I will do until Man turns his heart again to that which I seeded in his spirit, even before flesh was formed upon the earthly plane. Man will come to know it is I who granted the soul a purpose, and as such, each shall take part to preserve the surface of the Earth and the depths of the human spirit.

Bibliography

T he following texts were used as reference guides to verify identities, correct spellings, historical veracity and functions of The Iyrin named in this book.

Laurence, R. (1883). *The Book of Enoch The Prophet*, Translated from An Ethiopic Manuscript in the Bodleian Library. London: Kegan Paul, Trench & Co.

Davidson, G. (1971). *A Dictionary of Angels, Including the Fallen angels*. (New York, NY: The Free Press), 238-240.

Afterward

For over forty years, I have been contacted by and subsequently channeling, a group of fourteen sentient beings I have come to refer to as "The Council". It was from them that I was first told of *The Iyrin* – I was eight years old. I had never in my life, heard the word *Iyrin* before and was told by these beings, it was *"an ancient word given for the tongues of man"*, a word I had no expectation of ever coming across or knowing. After doing some research, I found that the word *Iyrin* did indeed have a meaning; it was/*is* a word meant to delineate Watchers from Heaven.

After years of privately chronicling the messages, insights and predictions I have received (and continue to receive), and given recent global events, the time had come for me to put aside my pride and fears of public ridicule. What you have read is only the beginnings of what *The Iyrin* have asked me to relay. I only pray I have not waited too long and that there is still time for those who *will* hear *to* hear. I give thanks to God for believing in me and guiding me. Valerie Jones, for being the living embodiment of strength and generosity. And a special heartfelt "thank you" to those who knew the truth of my burden, (which many would be quick to call a "gift", but have not had to bear). Thank you for giving me the courage, space, time, and in some cases, *years* to complete this project.

- *Nicole NiBlack Montoya*

About The Author

Nicole NiBlack Montoya is a native of Chicago, IL who resides in Northern Wisconsin, off the coastal shores of Lake Michigan with her husband Aldred and their wolfdog NaiLeiSha.

She and Aldred divide their time between the Midwest and the San Carlos Apache Reservation in Arizona.

Email: TheIyrinChronicles@gmail.com

CPSIA information can be obtained
at www.ICGtesting.com
Printed in the USA
LVHW020940030621
689238LV00004B/147